DO YOUR BEST
COACHING

THE
WORKBOOK

JULIE HESS & LAURA DALEY

ACKNOWLEDGMENTS

In April 2022 we celebrated the publication of *Do Your Best Coaching: Navigating A Coaching Engagement From Start To Finish*, and we have been deeply moved by the response from new and experienced coaches around the world. We are grateful for the conversations, relationships, and insights that have emerged from the experience, and for the knowledge that our book is supporting coaches to do their best work.

We are also grateful to be supported by an amazing community of family, friends, colleagues, and professionals who have offered their wisdom and support every step of the way.

To our early readers: Ann O'Connor, Anne McCune, Eric Paul, Gary Nowak, Julia Holloway, Michael Thaxton, and Paige Hinkson. Thank you for the gift of your time, care and deep attention. Your thoroughness and thoughtfulness are reflected in these pages.

To our supervision colleagues who have supported us throughout this journey: Alexis Chamow, Brenda Routt, Carol Tisson, DeAnne Aussem, Debbie Daniels, Francine Campone, Leanne Lowish, Janet Boguch, Joy Leach, Julia Holloway, Kathleen Stinnett, Kathryn Downing, Leslie Goldenberg, Lisa Johnson, Liz Congdon, Michelle Bastock, Mike Engsberg, Romi Boucher, Russ Hall, Ruth Williamson, Sarah Evans, Susan Geear, Trish Anastos.

To our fabulous colleagues who supported us along the way: Amira Leifer, Amy Jen Su, David Peck, Deb Gerardi, Kathy Gallo, Keith Naber, Kelly Ross, Melissa Hammer, Meredith Persily, Michael Hudson, Muriel Maignan Wilkins, Nancy Liffmann, Pam McLean, Pat Henahan, Sandy Smith, Seth Levenson, Suzanne Coonan, Taylor Keller.

To our amazing team: Alex Strathdee, Bethany Kelly, Catherine Knepper, Frank Steele, Irena Powers, Stefan Merour. Thank you for your expertise, patience, and commitment to excellence. We feel privileged to have worked with and learned from the best!

To our clients. It's an honor and privilege to do the deeply connected work of coaching with you, and to learn and grow alongside you. This book reflects our work together and would not have been possible without you.

Finally, to Dan, Alec and Maddie, who've loved and supported us along this journey even when it was challenging to do so, thank you. And now each of you is thinking about a time when that was true. And now each of you is thinking about another time when that was true...

We continue to be blessed to be part of so many vibrant coaching communities. We have had so many formal and informal teachers throughout the years that we cannot possibly include everyone here. We are grateful for every interaction, discussion, and connection, large and small.

Thank you.

Julie and Laura

CONTENTS

START HERE

If you have not read *Do Your Best Coaching: Navigating A Coaching Engagement From Start To Finish* (AKA *DYBC*, and really, what are you waiting for?), then let's start with its genesis and its connection to this workbook. And, if you have read *DYBC*, feel free to jump ahead to the next section entitled "How to Use This Workbook."

DYBC was born in the summer of 2020, during a conversation about the sticky situations we faced early in our coaching careers (and still do from time to time). Every coach has experienced sticky situations—challenges that distract from the actual coaching or that lead to disconnects. For example, a sponsor challenging you on confidentiality or an engagement ending without a true closing process. Sticky situations happen to everyone; and the problem is that they drain your energy and get in the way of doing the impactful coaching work you want to be doing with your client.

That summer our discussion expanded to the processes, conversations, and tools we had developed to prevent sticky situations and support healthy coaching engagements—things such as an intake process and kickoff meeting, clear communication and boundaries with sponsors, a compelling vision and coaching plan, and a meaningful closing process. We realized that when we approached an engagement intentionally from the start, and consistently integrated these elements across the arc of a coaching engagement, we created the container necessary to build a meaningful coaching relationship and do the deeply connected work we believe leads to great client outcomes. And, as a bonus, the risk of finding ourselves in a sticky situation was greatly reduced.

Almost simultaneously, we wished aloud that we'd had a practical guide outlining this approach when we were beginning our coaching practices. We laughed and said we could write that book now and title it *We Made Mistakes So You Don't Have To*!

Well, over time the title changed, but the book we wrote is true to that early wish. *DYBC* walks coaches through a coaching engagement from start to finish, sharing the best practices, processes, and tools pulled from our collective 30+ years of experience, along with insights from emerging research about the field of coaching as well as extensive firsthand interviews with dozens of new and experienced coaches.

And, over the years we have benefited from many coaches who have generously shared tools with us. And over the years we have adapted these and shared them with others, who have then surely evolved and passed them along. Therefore, we want to acknowledge that the tools and practices included in this workbook have their roots in a collective community of work, and for that we are grateful.

Here's where the workbook comes in. While writing *DYBC*, we built a robust appendix full of tools, checklists, and other useful resources, and *DYBC* grew and grew, becoming significantly longer than was practical. Early readers encouraged us to "right-size" our use of examples and compile all of the structures, checklists, templates, and coaching exercises into an easy-to-access reference. Thus, *Do Your Best Coaching: The Workbook* was born, a practical companion to *DYBC*.

We have endeavored to create a workbook that can stand on its own without exhaustively repeating the content of our initial book. However, like most companions (e.g., peanut butter and jelly, mac and cheese), the two volumes are better together than on their own. So, if you are exploring *DYBC: The Workbook* and find yourself wanting to know more, we encourage you to pick up a copy of *DYBC* for a deeper dive into any of the topics covered. You won't regret it!

THE INTENTIONAL ENGAGEMENT FRAMEWORK & SUPPORTING PROCESSES

WHY INTENTIONAL ENGAGEMENT MATTERS

ntentional engagement is the act of mindfully and consistently attending to the processes and tools that support a healthy coaching engagement. As the framing of a building creates the structure that holds the space in the rooms, intentional engagement *creates the space for the coaching relationship, and the coaching conversations that take place within it*. And, like framing, it is not what you should see when you look at a coaching engagement. When done well, intentional engagement runs seamlessly in the background, creating the container for you to do your best coaching.

Our Intentional Engagement Framework helps you build the container that best serves your particular practice and supports you in navigating the overall flow and direction of each coaching engagement. Below we explore the four phases of the Intentional Engagement Framework, and identify its seven supporting components.

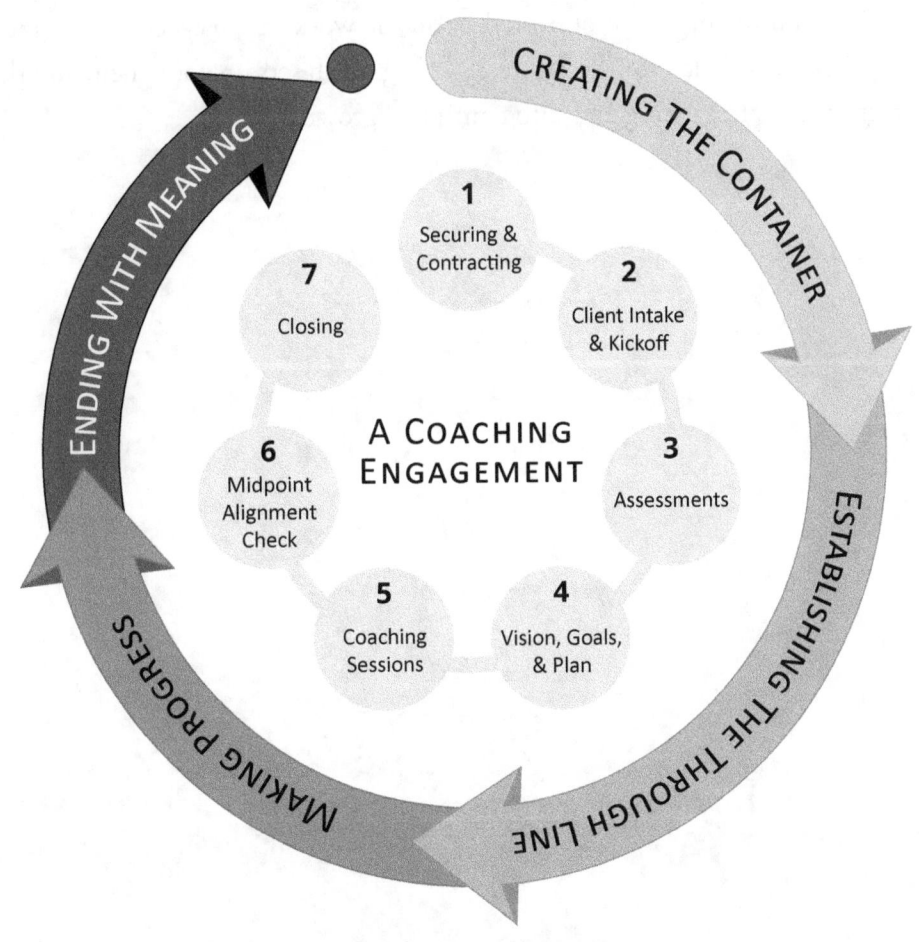

CREATING THE CONTAINER

ESTABLISHING THE THROUGH LINE

MAKING PROGRESS

ENDING WITH MEANING

1 Securing & Contracting

2 Client Intake & Kickoff

3 Assessments

4 Vision, Goals, & Plan

5 Coaching Sessions

6 Midpoint Alignment Check

7 Closing

A COACHING ENGAGEMENT

THE INTENTIONAL ENGAGEMENT FRAMEWORK

PHASE I: CREATING THE CONTAINER

Defining ways of working with your client and the organization, including establishing boundaries and confidentiality, all of which are essential to developing the safe space and trust required in a healthy coaching relationship.

PHASE II: ESTABLISHING THE THROUGH LINE

Clarifying where your client is today, what future success looks like personally and professionally, and the changes that will help them get from here to there. Establishing a through line ensures alignment on coaching objectives and creates the freedom to pivot to emerging issues when necessary, without losing focus.

PHASE III: MAKING PROGRESS

Coaching clients as they work to make the changes they aspire to, while checking for alignment with both your client and the sponsor throughout the process. Great coaching coupled with alignment touchpoints leads to clarity regarding success and client progress.

PHASE IV: ENDING WITH MEANING

Supporting your client and the organization to reflect on the work that has been done, identify and celebrate your client's progress, and plan for the future. A strong finish sets up your client and the organization for a smooth transition out of coaching and into continued growth.

HOW TO USE THIS WORKBOOK

Like *DYBC*, this workbook follows the arc of a coaching engagement from start to finish, using the Intentional Engagement Framework (IEF) to illustrate the tools and processes we use, and why we use them. It is oriented to a coaching engagement conducted by an external coach within an organization. This approach enables us to cover the spectrum of roles, tools, and complexities that occur in this type of work. However, we know that many coaches also work directly with clients or are internal coaches. If this is the case for you, choose and integrate what's useful into your particular practice, based on your style and preferences, the work you do, and the clients you serve.

The book is organized into the four phases of the IEF. Within each phase are chapters that focus on a specific component of the coaching process (e.g., Building Awareness: Assessments). Each chapter begins with a process graphic that illustrates the steps for you, your client, and the sponsor, as seen in the example below:

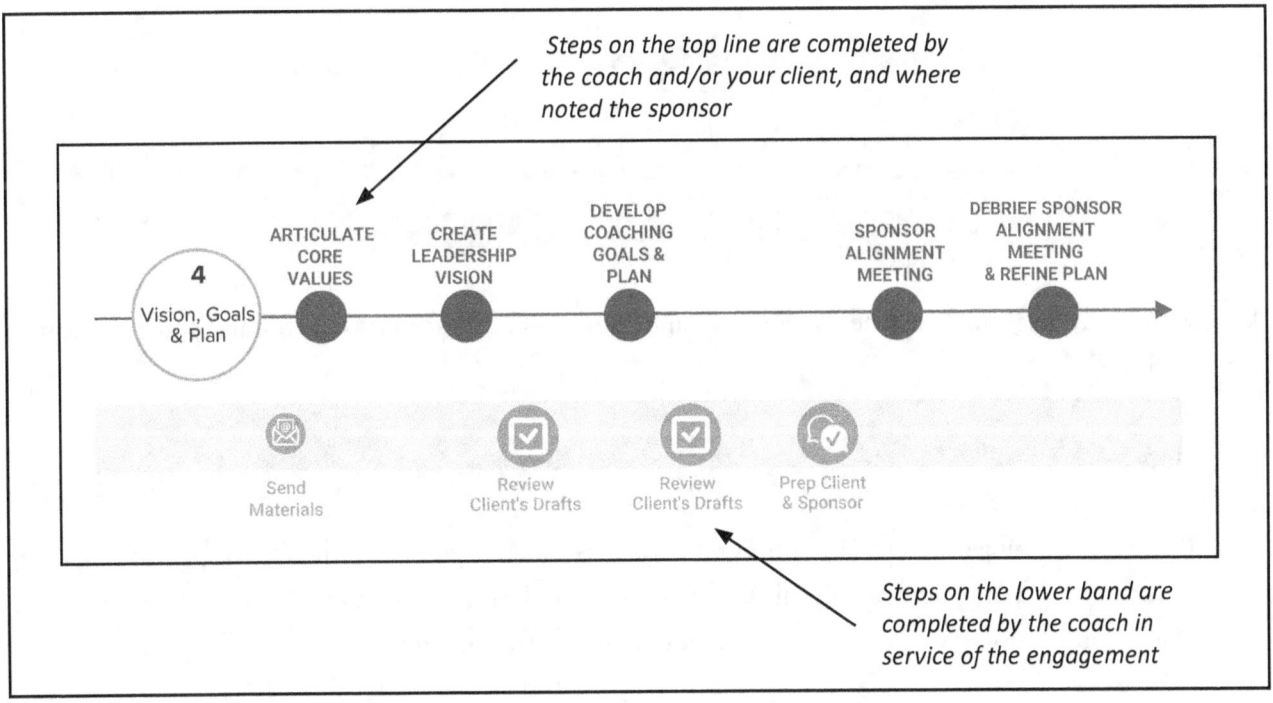

We then dive into the following:

- The key outcomes you want to achieve
- Checklists organized to capture the flow and detail of activities
- Tools, templates, and examples to support these activities
- Sticky situations related to this part of the engagement, and
- A place for you to reflect and integrate, capturing your insights and next steps.

We know we do our best work when we are intentional about ourselves as coaches. So, in addition to offering the client-facing tools and processes we use across the arc of an engagement, we have provided opportunities for you to pause and reflect on who you are as a coach at the beginning and end of the workbook.

Building the Foundation—Coach Self-Reflections invites you to consider who you are as a coach today and to develop an intentional vision for your future, including the work you wish to be doing and the clients you wish to engage with.

After the Engagement provides an opportunity to consider your overall development, including your presence as a coach, as well as a holistic approach to deepening your coaching capabilities.

Finally, there are times we draw attention to a topic that is covered in greater depth in *DYBC*. In these instances, we have used this icon to make it easy for you to find these opportunities.

PRACTICAL APPLICATIONS

We invite you to use this workbook as a practical resource—consider what's useful and integrate it into your coaching.

For example:

- If you are thinking generally about **how you work as a coach**, start with the *IEF Self-Assessment for Coaches* in the Appendix, a helpful starting point to reflect on your current approach and consider where you are doing well and where you would benefit from increased intentionality.

- If you are coming to this workbook with **a specific client engagement in mind**, you may wish to go directly to the chapter that mirrors the place you are in that engagement. For example, if you are working with your client to develop coaching goals, go to Chapter 4: Charting the Course: Coaching Plans—Vision and Goal Setting.

- If you are thinking about **your own development as a coach**, you might start with Chapter 9: You Are Your Own Best Tool: Ongoing Development for Coaches.

BUILDING THE FOUNDATION
COACH SELF-REFLECTIONS

As coaches we spend a lot of time helping our clients to reflect on who they are today and to create a compelling vision for the future. And, despite our best intentions, sometimes we are less likely to take the time to engage in this reflective practice for ourselves.

Creating this clarity for ourselves provides a useful foundation that can be applied in many ways. For example, coaches are often asked to share their coaching approach and philosophy during an initial inquiry conversation or in a chemistry meeting with a potential client. And, just as we coach our clients, developing a compelling vision for our own future can help us identify the shifts necessary to fuel our development plans and achieve our goals.

We invite you to pause, reflect, and answer the questions below.

Please do not rush through this exercise. Consider working on it in various segments over time, refining your responses as you reflect on past situations, personal feelings, and what inspires you as you look to the future.

This is a living document that you will revisit and update over time, serving as a reminder to focus on your own growth and to be as intentional with yourself as you are with your clients.

WHO AM I AS A COACH TODAY?
What is my coaching philosophy?

What are my strengths as a coach?

What are my learning edges?

WHO DO I WANT TO BE AS A COACH IN THE FUTURE?

What aspects of my coaching philosophy do I wish to evolve?

What strengths do I want to bring forward?

What types of development will support my intentional growth?

HOW DO I WORK AS A COACH TODAY?

Reflect back on the past 12 months as you answer the following questions:

What is important to me about my current coaching approach?

What is important to my clients about this approach?

What do I like about my current coaching process/approach?

Where did I do my best work? What made it my best, and what conditions enabled it?

What, if any, recurring sticky situations did I face that could be prevented or minimized by altering my approach?

What does my portfolio of work look like (e.g., types of work, organizations and/or leaders)?

What clients do I most enjoy working with? Why?

What clients do I prefer to avoid? Why?

What types of organizations do I most enjoy working with? Why?

What types of organizations do I prefer to avoid? Why?

Do I have the right amount of work and/or number of clients to have a meaningful and sustainable coaching practice consistent with the life I want to lead?

HOW DO I WANT TO WORK AS A COACH IN THE FUTURE?
What would I like to change or experiment with in my current process/approach?

Are there any new coaching modalities or tools that I'd like to explore? If so, what draws me to them?

What types of clients or organizations am I feeling drawn to?

Am I feeling "done" with any particular types of clients or organizations? If so, what types or organizations?

How might I want to increase or decrease the amount of work and/or number of clients I have in order to have a meaningful and sustainable coaching practice consistent with the life I want to lead?

ENVISION YOUR FUTURE
What do I want my life to look like in the years ahead?

How does work fit into that vision?

Who do I want to be as a coach in the years ahead?

What type of work do I want to be doing, with whom, and where?

NOW CREATE YOUR VISION STATEMENT

Once you have created a compelling vision of your desired future as a coach, capture the essence of it in a sentence or two. Below is an example you can use as a model.

Vision Statement Example

I work with vibrant leaders and changemakers who are passionate about growing their impact and leading their organizations to new heights of excellence. My clients love learning, are willing to experiment in order to grow, and work with me for 6- to 12-month engagements.

Date: January 13, 2023

My Vision Statement:

If you want to make this reflection a regular part of your work, we provide additional worksheets in the Appendix and at DoYourBestCoaching.com.

PHASE I
CREATING THE CONTAINER

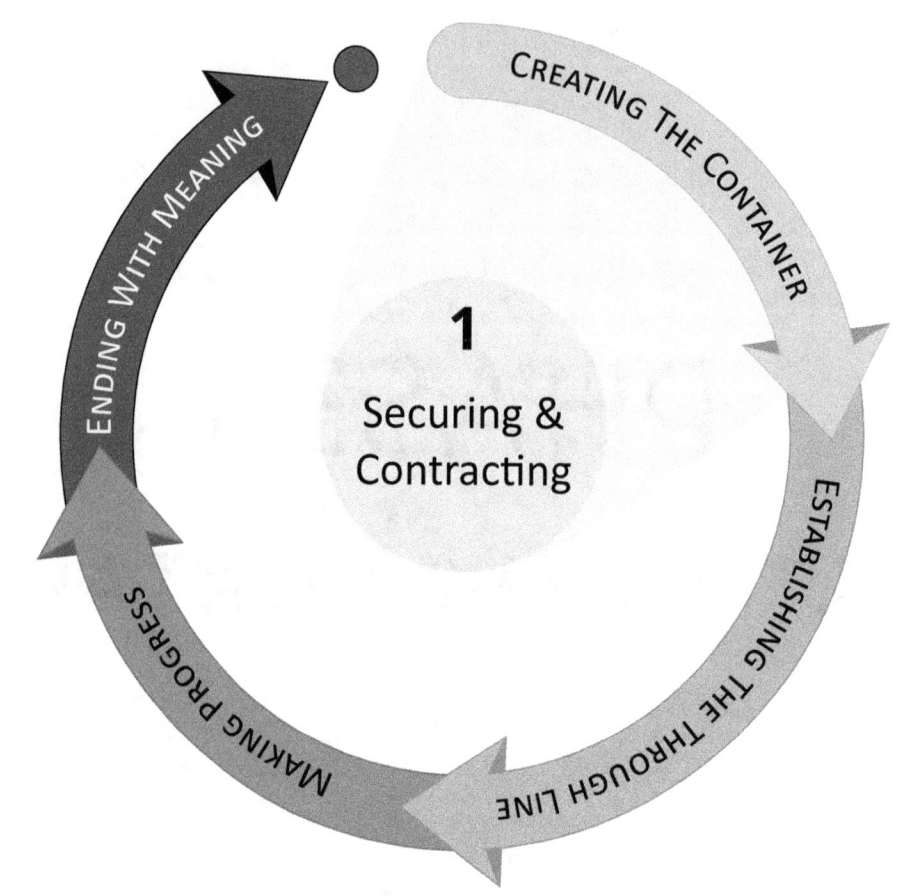

CHAPTER 1

PUTTING YOUR BEST FOOT FORWARD: SECURING & CONTRACTING AN ENGAGEMENT

The first step in securing and contracting an engagement is typically an initial inquiry discussion. If the initial inquiry originates from someone other than the potential client (e.g., a hiring contact or sponsor), it is then followed by a chemistry call to assess fit. If you and the client decide to move forward, a Statement of Work (SOW) is developed and agreed upon. How you handle the initial inquiry discussion and chemistry meeting is important, not just to secure the engagement, but to set the tone and establish expectations for the engagement to follow. A clear SOW further establishes the structure and boundaries of the engagement.

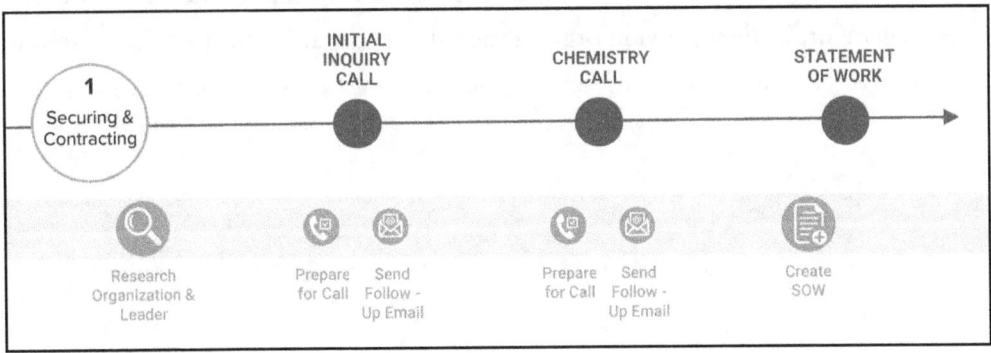

KEY OUTCOMES
SECURING AND CONTRACTING AN ENGAGEMENT

- Boundaries and confidentiality to enable safety and candor with the client and the organization
- Alignment on the coaching process and roles and responsibilities at your client and organizational level to facilitate smooth engagement
- Agreed documentation on how the engagement will be conducted, such as coaching activities, alignment meetings, confidentiality, and payment
- The foundation necessary for an impactful, trusting coaching relationship

Below we define the roles and responsibilities of an engagement when the organization has hired a coach on behalf of the client. However, if a client hires you directly, they serve as both the hiring contact and the client, and there will not be a sponsor involved.

Hiring Contact. An individual who makes the initial request for the coaching engagement and serves as a point of contact for administration, such as creating the SOW and invoicing. This role can be filled by the client or the client's manager, but is often filled by someone in Human Resources (HR), Talent Management (TM), or Learning and Development (L&D). In large organizations, you may work with an individual hiring contact for many coaching engagements. If you are working with an individual directly, that person is also the hiring contact.

Client. The person who is being coached.

Engagement Sponsor. In corporate engagements, this is the individual who is championing and supporting the client through the engagement. The client's manager often plays this role; however, if HR is involved, an HR leader may share in certain aspects of it. Sponsors play an important role in a coaching engagement, as they provide organizational context and direction for coaching objectives, as well as feedback and support during the coaching process.

INITIAL
INQUIRY
CALL

CHEMISTRY
CALL

STATEMENT
OF WORK

1
Securing &
Contracting

PUTTING YOUR BEST FOOT FORWARD

MY NOTES:

THE INITIAL INQUIRY AND CHEMISTRY CALLS

CHECKLIST: PREPARING FOR CALLS

☐ Do a capacity check. Do you have time to begin a new client engagement immediately? If not now, when will you be available to begin? How will you share this information with the prospective client? For a detailed discussion on managing your capacity, see DYBC Chapter 5.

☐ Review and refresh yourself on questions you may wish to ask (1-1), as well as questions you may be asked during these calls (1-2).

☐ Research the organization, its industry, competitors, and recent events using online tools and resources.

☐ Research your client (typically after an inquiry call and in advance of a chemistry call), using tools such as the organization's website and online tools like LinkedIn.

☐ Schedule time prior to the call to revisit the information you gathered about the organization and your client; also reserve time on your calendar immediately before the call to center yourself energetically.

☐ Confirm that your coaching bio is up to date so you can share it easily with the potential client prior to the call (1-3).

☐ If you share a sample engagement list, include any experiences relevant to your client (1-4).

☐ Be prepared to offer a general approach to the call (1-5) and to share an overview of your coaching process. If you use a coaching process document (1-6), ensure that it is easily accessible for your call.

☐ Spend several minutes getting present before the call (1-7) so that you enter the discussion with intentionality and bring your best and most authentic self forward.

TOOLS, TEMPLATES, AND EXAMPLES

1-1 QUESTIONS YOU MAY WISH TO ASK DURING AN INQUIRY CALL

COACH CONSIDERATION: In addition to assessing fit, you will also be assessing the potential client's coaching readiness. For example, is your client's issue coachable? If so, are they ready to do the work at this time? Finally, do they have the necessary support of the organization for this work?

COACH CONSIDERATION: In addition, you will be assessing the organization's perception and usage of coaching/coaches, which can provide you with insights valuable to your coaching efforts and even help you decide whether the organization is right for you.

WHEN TALKING TO THE POTENTIAL CLIENT	WHEN TALKING TO THE HIRING CONTACT OR SPONSOR
Tell me about yourself and what's motivating you to seek a coach right now. What might you want to work on with a coach?	Tell me about the potential client. What are the development objectives that have been identified and targeted for their coaching?
	How has coaching been positioned with the potential client? How did they respond?
What feedback have you received from your manager or anyone else in the organization? How did you feel about the feedback?	Has the organization provided any feedback to the client to date? If so, how did the client respond to the feedback?
What development support have you received from your company to date?	What type of development support, if any, has your client received to date?
What does your organization need from you in terms of business goals and performance in the next 6–12 months?	What does the organization need from this leader in terms of business goals and performance in the next 6–12 months?
What's your experience with, or perception of, coaching?	How does the organization feel about and use coaching (e.g., accelerating development of high performers or "fixing" underperformers)?
What role do you anticipate the organization playing in your coaching?	What role do you anticipate the organization playing in the coaching?
What cultural norms do I need to be aware of so I can support you most effectively?	What organizational norms do I need to be aware of so I can be as effective as possible (e.g., is informal feedback a generally accepted practice in your organization)?
Other Questions You May Wish to Ask:	Other Questions You May Wish to Ask:
_____	_____
Other:	Other:
_____	_____

1-2 QUESTIONS YOU SHOULD BE PREPARED TO ANSWER DURING AN INQUIRY OR CHEMISTRY CALL

- Walk me through your coaching process.

- What's your coaching philosophy?

- Have you worked with clients in my industry/function/situation before?

- Can you give me examples of working with someone in my role or with similar goals?

- Tell me about a coaching engagement that went well.

- Tell me about a coaching engagement that didn't go well.

- What makes for a successful coaching engagement?

- How do you measure success?

- How much of my time will coaching take?

- What's it like to work with you?

- I'm not exactly sure why I have been asked to engage in coaching right now. Do you have any information you can share with me?

- What is your typical fee for a coaching engagement?

Other questions I want to be prepared for:

- _____?

- _____?

COACH CONSIDERATION: Listen for clues that your client may be looking for advising, consulting, or mentoring in addition to coaching. Use this as an opportunity to explain the difference between these types of support and gain alignment on the work you will be doing together.

COACH CONSIDERATION: Sometimes potential clients come to chemistry calls without knowing why coaching is being suggested for them and may ask you directly about what you've been told. If this is the case, encourage the potential client to ask their sponsor directly for feedback, and to describe from their perspective what successful coaching outcomes would be.

1-3 COACH BIOGRAPHY

> **COACH CONSIDERATION:** Many coaches include a professional headshot and a link to their LinkedIn profile in their coaching biography.

Andie Carlson

1-222-333-4444

andie.carlson@carlsoncoaching.com

Andie Carlson coaches executive and mid-career leaders to maximize their impact and realize their fullest potential by making purpose-driven changes that empower them to become the best leaders they can be. Her coaching style is upbeat and supportive yet firm, and focuses on helping leaders incorporate their authentic way of being into how they lead.

Andie's 20-year corporate career prior to coaching gives her a unique ability to empathize and engage with leaders at all levels, enabling the mutual trust and respect that is the foundation of an effective coaching relationship. Clients appreciate her keen insight into the complexity of organizations, her challenging questions, and her unconditional positive regard.

Andie works with clients to bring forth:

- Greater self-awareness, including their values and an aspirational vision for the future
- A clear understanding of what they want to gain from coaching
- Organizational alignment with their coaching agenda and success
- A plan to put the change in place
- Practices and reflections to support new mindsets, skills, and behaviors to achieve their goals

She often works with executives in the areas of increasing executive presence, demonstrating strategic capability, and inspiring and developing teams, among others.

Professional Experience and Qualifications

Andie spent ten years as an organizational design consultant working across industries and geographies to help create the organizational structures and human capital capabilities that support her clients' strategic goals. Her previous experience includes moving up the ladder in the marketing organization of a Fortune 500 consumer products company. Right out of school, she participated in a management rotation program at an industrial materials firm.

Andie has a BA from TBU College and completed her coach training at The Institute of Leadership Coaching. She's certified in numerous assessments and is constantly pursuing new knowledge and skills to bring to her coaching work.

1-4 RECENT COACHING ENGAGEMENTS

Some coaches include this information in their bio; others leave it as a separate document, depending on how they like to share their materials with others.

Andie Carlson: Recent Coaching Engagements

- CEO of a national financial services company, to improve leadership effectiveness, facilitate team development, and strengthen communication with the board
- Chief Product Officer at a SAS technology company, to shift focus from operational to strategic issues and better influence executive peers
- CHRO of an executive search firm to successfully transition into a new role as leader of a global HR team
- CIO of a consumer products company, to better develop and motivate team members and lead a significant IT transformation effort
- Business Unit President at an equipment manufacturer to lead more strategically and inclusively
- EVP of a global financial services company, to prepare for and successfully transition into the CEO role
- Vice President of marketing at a pharmaceutical company, to support a successful transition into an expanded role with a focus on leading more strategically
- Partner at a public consulting firm, to hone business development skills and better leverage teams

> COACH CONSIDERATION: Be guided by confidentiality agreements or constraints when deciding whether to include names of organizations or specific titles in your list of recent coaching engagements.

1-5 CHEMISTRY CALL APPROACH

While we do not share a formal agenda prior to a chemistry call, we often offer the potential client a suggested flow. For example:

Coach:
"This time is for you, so I want to make sure you get what you need. If you can share what is most important for you to cover today, I am happy to suggest an approach."

Potential Client: Shares what they are hoping to discuss

"Let me suggest that we spend some time getting to know each other. Then we can discuss what's bringing you to coaching and your hopes for it. I'd also like to hear about any coaching experiences you have had, and I am happy to share my coaching process and how we might work together. How does that sound to you?"

MY NOTES:

During the conversation, ask questions (1-1) to shape the conversation. There may also be an opportunity to help your client understand the experience of coaching. You can do this by talking through what is bringing them to coaching, or you can offer light coaching on an issue that surfaces during the conversation. While this can be very helpful for both coach and client, we are careful not to force this into the discussion.

1-6 COACHING PROCESS OVERVIEW

This is a client-facing document we often use to walk a client or sponsor through the coaching engagement. It illustrates the arc of the engagement, what we do (actions), and why we do it (outcomes).

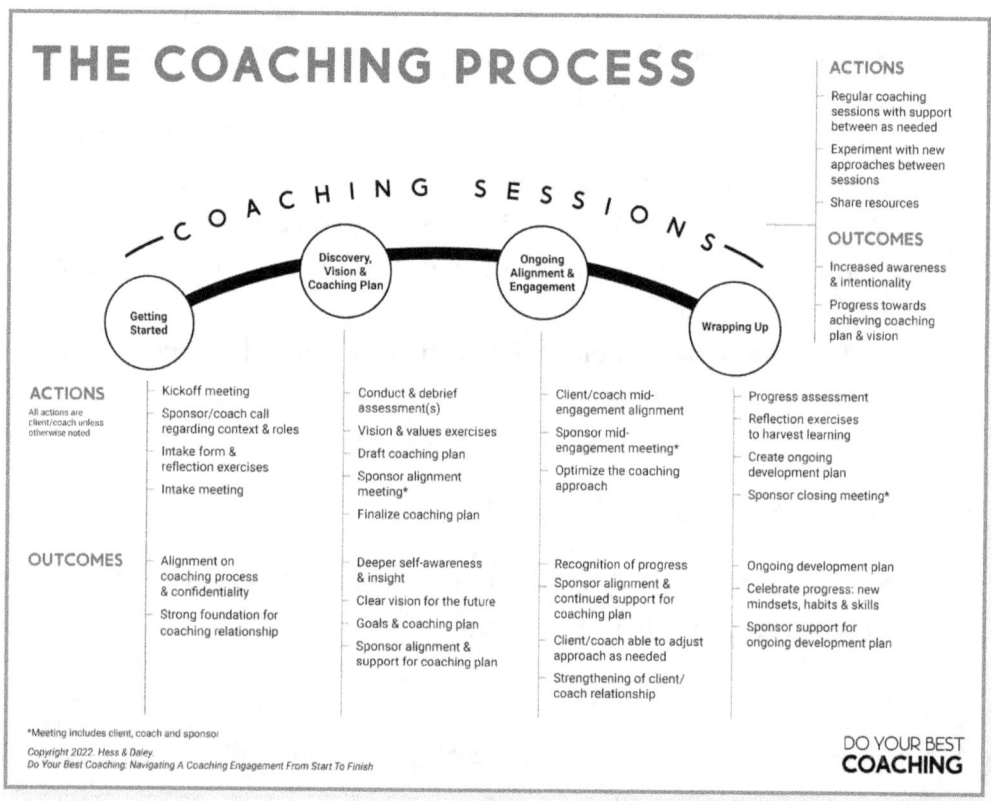

You can download a color version of this coaching process document at doyourbestcoaching.com

1-7 GETTING PRESENT BEFORE THE CALL

As the call approaches, make time to revisit the research you have done. Then, as you would with any client session, make time to relax and get present ahead of an inquiry or chemistry call. Here are a few ways to do that. You'll also find additional practices in Chapter 8 of this workbook.

Visualization

Imagine you are at the end of the call, and it went great. Consider some aspects that contributed to its success. How did you imagine yourself doing the following:

- Starting the call
- Engaging with the person during the call
- Managing your energy during the call
- Ending the call

With this clarity in mind, take a few moments to align your energy and intention to the insights you gained from your visualization.

Breathwork

With eyes open, softened, or closed, tune in to your breathing. Take deep inhalations to fill your belly, lungs, and chest, followed by slow, complete exhalations. Repeat 3–5 times.

Embodiment

Inhale and grow tall, exhale, and expand your heart area. Bring to mind several characteristics you want to bring to this conversation (e.g., compassion, curiosity…). Bring to mind someone who embodies these characteristics, and assume the shape of that person. Smile.

CHECKLIST: POST-CALL FOLLOW-UP

- ☐ Reflect on the conversation and capture your insights and learnings, as well as any agreements and next steps (1-8).

- ☐ Share any documents that will help your client, hiring contact, or sponsor understand the coaching engagement (e.g., coaching bio, coaching process…).

- ☐ Send a thank-you email expressing interest and asking any follow-up questions, such as the timing of the decision.

- ☐ Put a future date reminder on your calendar to prompt a check-in with the individual if you have not yet heard back from them.

TOOLS, TEMPLATES, AND EXAMPLES

1-8 POST-CALL REFLECTION QUESTIONS

Once you have completed the call, pause and reflect on the fit:

- Is this the right type of client and/or organization for me right now?
- Does the timing of the engagement work well for me, or will it be a challenge (e.g., too many simultaneous clients starting in a short time frame)?
- What did I notice about my energy during the call?
- Am I excited about the prospect of working with this client/organization?
- If I'm trying to focus my practice on a new direction: Is this client/organization consistent with the direction I am moving as a coach, or is it more consistent with how I have always worked?
- If I'm clear that this is not a client and/or organization that I wish to work with at this time, can I think of coaches that I could offer as referrals?

> COACH CONSIDERATION: If this is a potential client that does not feel like a great fit, consider getting in touch with the hiring contact to share your experience of the call and, if you have them, offer referrals.

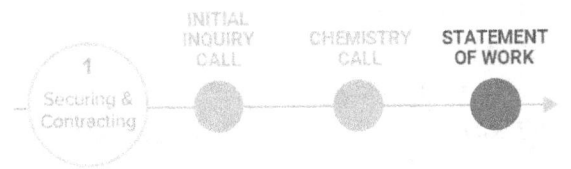

CREATING A STATEMENT OF WORK (SOW)

The term contracting is used in multiple ways to describe both formal and informal agreements that occur throughout the course of a coaching engagement. For clarity we use the following definition to describe this type of contracting:

Statement of Work (SOW). The formal, legal agreement a coach enters into with the client or the client's organization.

CHECKLIST: DRAFT THE SOW

☐ Confirm that you have the correct information for the SOW, including who it should be addressed to, where you should send it, and the timing.

☐ Before drafting the SOW, verbally confirm your approach with the hiring contact in order to avoid over- or under-delivering.

☐ Inquire about any organization-specific language or requirements that need to be addressed.

☐ Draft the SOW (1-9).

☐ Review (1-10), finalize, and send the SOW to the appropriate individual (e.g., client, hiring contact, or engagement sponsor).

☐ Follow up as needed so each party has a signed, completed SOW.

TOOLS, TEMPLATES, AND EXAMPLES

1-9 DRAFT THE SOW

We have a standard SOW that we customize based on the client and their organization, which includes:

- Objectives for the coaching engagement
- Duration of the coaching engagement and number of meetings within this time frame.
- Key elements of your coaching process, including:
  - How meetings will be conducted (e.g., in person, by phone, by videoconference, a hybrid)
  - Assessments you have agreed to conduct (e.g., 360°) and how other assessments may be used
  - How you will keep the engagement sponsor informed and how you will ensure organizational alignment (e.g., alignment meetings with sponsor and client)
- Confidentiality for all coaching sessions and assessment reports
- Cost of the engagement and expense policy
- Payment terms

Because there are infinite approaches to writing an SOW, driven by coach preference, organizational needs, and the legal system in which you are working, we have not included an example of a standard SOW. We recommend you use examples provided by coach accreditation bodies, a coaching colleague, or your coach certification program.

While we hope this never happens, SOWs can be forwarded to others in the organization beyond the hiring contact. So we assume that the SOW could be seen by anyone, and are careful to frame the objectives in a manner that safeguards the reputation of the client, regardless of the audience. At times we may even use generic outcomes such as "increased self-awareness; new skills, mindsets, and practices; and progress against the coaching goals to be determined early in the engagement."

1-10 SOW REVIEW QUESTIONS

Prior to sending an SOW, we do a final review and ask the following questions:

- Do I have any last-minute questions or concerns that I should address prior to moving forward?
- Have I realistically assessed my capacity? If not and you need to delay the start, now is the time to have that conversation and develop an SOW that reflects this timing. Against our better judgment, we have both pushed forward with work we did not really have the capacity for to accommodate a client, and regretted it later.
- Have I structured compensation and a cancellation policy to match the flow of the work? For example, in an engagement with an interview-based 360° process, more of the work is front-loaded. For example:

Should the coaching engagement terminate prior to completion, the Company agrees to pay the fees scheduled above on a prorated basis based on the months of completed coaching as below. This reflects time and work invested by the coach:

Months 1-2: X% of total fees
Months 3-6: Y% of total fees

STICKY SITUATIONS THAT CAN OCCUR DURING SECURING AND CONTRACTING AN ENGAGEMENT

STICKY SITUATION	WHAT TO DO
You're concerned that an organization is asking you to coach in a way that is not aligned with the work you do. Examples include: • "Rescue mission" or "check the box" coaching • Abdicating responsibility for feedback and development • Advising or consulting camouflaged as coaching	Assess the level of organizational support for the potential client during the initial inquiry discussions. If you have any concerns, consider asking the sponsor directly why coaching is being considered and what the desired outcomes are. If you believe the proposed engagement is not for you, gracefully decline the request.
You're at or over capacity and a potential client wants to start right away.	Periodically review your client load and capacity and the impact of starting a new client. Is the time right, or would you and your client benefit from delaying the start? If you find you are over capacity, can you engage with the client on their timeframe—getting them started on self-reflection and early coaching, delaying any heavy lifting activities, such as an interview-based 360, by several weeks?

COACH CONSIDERATION: To prevent this situation in the future, monitor your capacity periodically as part of managing your practice. When you find yourself at capacity and interviewing for new engagements, identify a start date that would work for you. Be ready to communicate that to any potential client.

WAYS TO AVOID FUTURE STICKY SITUATIONS DURING INTAKE AND KICKOFF

STICKY SITUATION	HOW TO PREVENT
You feel pressure to start the engagement (kickoff and intake process) without a signed SOW.	Communicate directly to the individual managing the SOW process that you cannot begin coaching without a signed SOW.
You skipped aspects of intake and kickoff because your client needed to jump right into coaching but are now impacted by the missing information and relationship building.	Immediately after you receive the news that you have been selected for the engagement, send an email to your client with next steps for the kickoff and intake process. This signals to your client the importance of intake discussions during your initial meetings.

Many sticky situations occur because a client and/or sponsor does not fully understand the coaching process and/or the roles and responsibilities for the client, coach, and sponsor. If possible, share your coaching process and discuss roles and responsibilities in early discussions to proactively manage expectations.

RESOURCES

- To download a color pdf of the coaching process, go to: Doyourbestcoaching.com/resources/
- *Building a Coaching Business,* by Jenny Rogers (Open University Press, 2017)

YOUR TURN

HOW CAN YOU BRING MORE INTENTION TO SECURING AND CONTRACTING AN ENGAGEMENT?

Reflect on your current practices and the materials shared here.

1. What are you currently doing well?

2. Where would you like to develop, experiment, and/or learn more?

3. I am energized to experiment in these areas:

WHAT TOOLS AND PRACTICES WILL HELP YOU STRENGTHEN THIS ASPECT OF YOUR PRACTICE?

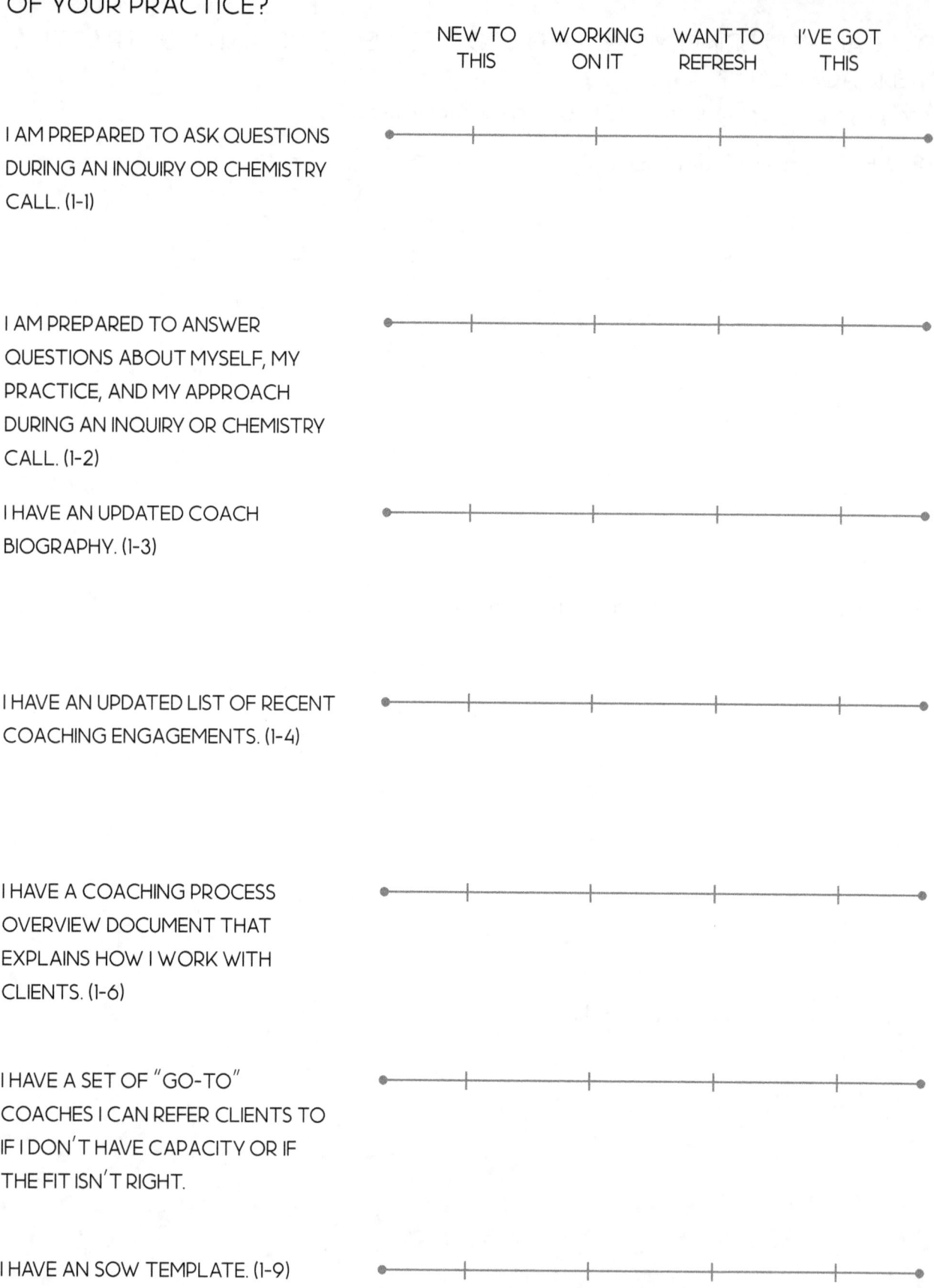

	NEW TO THIS	WORKING ON IT	WANT TO REFRESH	I'VE GOT THIS
I AM PREPARED TO ASK QUESTIONS DURING AN INQUIRY OR CHEMISTRY CALL. (1-1)				
I AM PREPARED TO ANSWER QUESTIONS ABOUT MYSELF, MY PRACTICE, AND MY APPROACH DURING AN INQUIRY OR CHEMISTRY CALL. (1-2)				
I HAVE AN UPDATED COACH BIOGRAPHY. (1-3)				
I HAVE AN UPDATED LIST OF RECENT COACHING ENGAGEMENTS. (1-4)				
I HAVE A COACHING PROCESS OVERVIEW DOCUMENT THAT EXPLAINS HOW I WORK WITH CLIENTS. (1-6)				
I HAVE A SET OF "GO-TO" COACHES I CAN REFER CLIENTS TO IF I DON'T HAVE CAPACITY OR IF THE FIT ISN'T RIGHT.				
I HAVE AN SOW TEMPLATE. (1-9)				

CREATE YOUR PLAN

NOTES		
TIMING		
NEXT STEPS		
TOOL OR APPROACH		

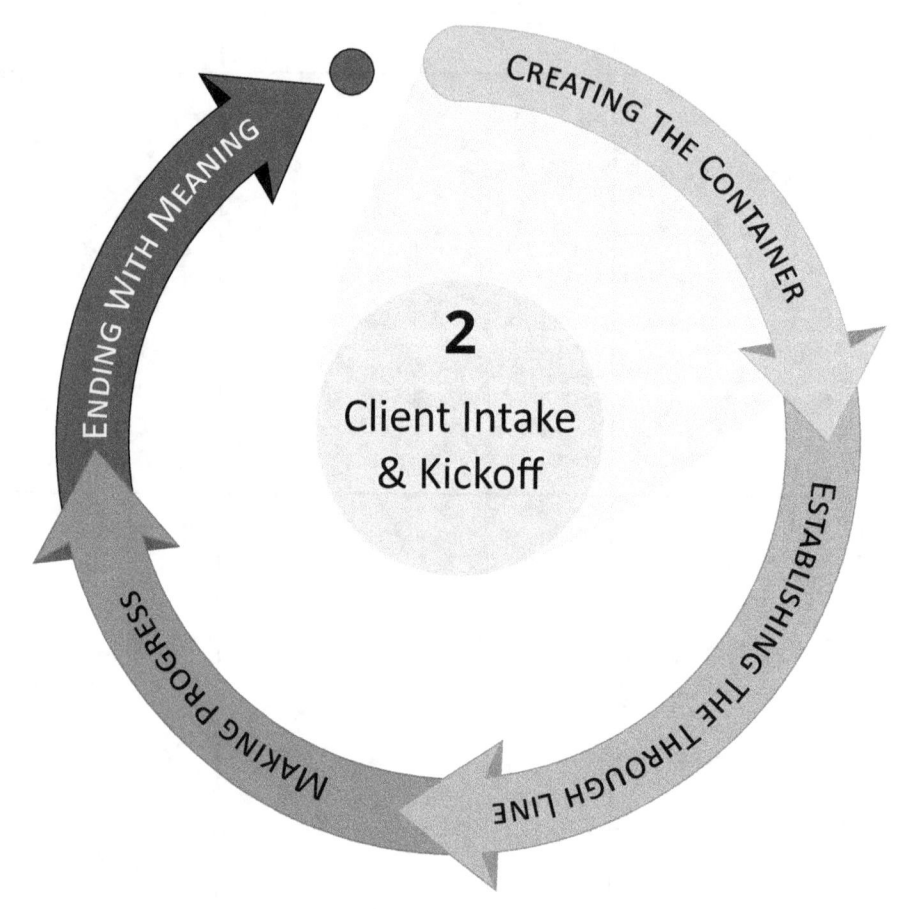

CREATING THE CONTAINER

ESTABLISHING THE THROUGH LINE

MAKING PROGRESS

ENDING WITH MEANING

2

Client Intake
& Kickoff

CHAPTER 2

STARTING STRONG:
CLIENT INTAKE & KICKOFF

The most robust inquiry discussions or chemistry meetings do not take the place of a well-managed kickoff and intake process. Throughout the kickoff and intake process, you continue **Creating the Container** for coaching, building a relationship with your new client while establishing the alignment and structure for your work together. Laying a strong foundation with clear processes, roles, and expectations can prevent unnecessary challenges and sticky situations later on.

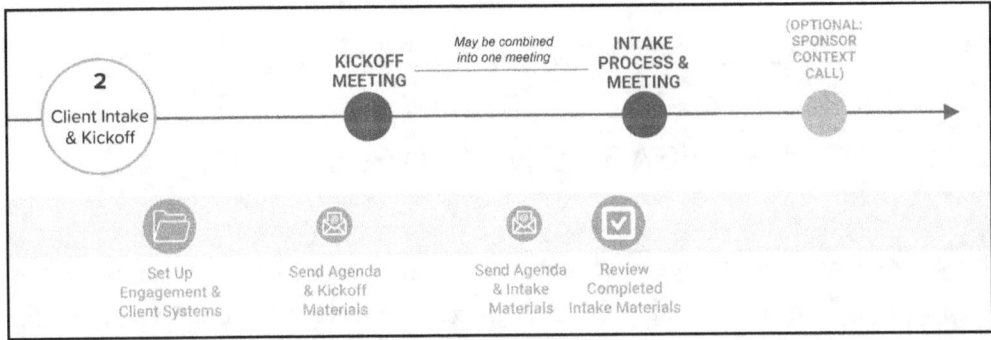

Note: While we make a clear distinction between the kickoff meeting, which is focused on how you will work together, and the first coaching session/intake meeting, which is when you will begin your work together, some coaches combine these meetings into a single session. Additionally, the sponsor context call is an optional component and may happen earlier in the process than illustrated above.

KEY OUTCOMES
CLIENT INTAKE AND KICKOFF

- Boundaries and confidentiality to enable safety and candor with the client and the organization
- Alignment on the coaching process, and roles and responsibilities at client and organizational level, to facilitate smooth engagement
- Clients shift to a coaching mindset
- The foundation necessary for an impactful, trusting coaching relationship

SET UP ENGAGEMENT AND CLIENT SYSTEMS

CHECKLIST: SET UP ENGAGEMENT AND CLIENT SYSTEMS

❑ Create a new client file, digital or analog, and start populating it prior to your first meeting (2-1).

❑ Set up your client in your financial systems.

❑ Tailor your standard welcome email (2-2) for this new client and send it once the SOW is signed; include an overview of Roles & Responsibilities (2-3), a Coaching Agreement (2-4), and a New Client Intake Form (2-5).

TOOLS, TEMPLATES, AND EXAMPLES

COACH CONSIDERATION: If using paper files, include a Post-It or sheet of paper on the inside cover of the file to track client interactions for easy, manual tracking of the engagement as you prepare for or reflect on each client meeting.

2-1 SET UP NEW ENGAGEMENT AND CLIENT FILE

Keeping client materials together in either a digital or analog file ensures we stay organized, and the integrated set of client materials also supports our preparation for client meetings. We set up this file prior to the kickoff meeting so that we don't find ourselves with information scattered in multiple places several sessions later. A typical new client file includes:

- Basic contact information for your client, sponsors, and EAs
- Preferred mode of communication (email, text, call, etc.)
- Important dates (board or leadership team meetings, vacations, etc.)
- Prior assessment information shared by the client
- A copy of the SOW
- A checklist of key milestones
- Session tracker
- As the engagement progresses: the Leadership Vision, Coaching Goals and Plan, key insights and reflections, shared resources, and completed assessments

TOOLS, TEMPLATES, AND EXAMPLES

2-2 WELCOME AND GETTING STARTED EMAIL

From: Andie Carlson <andie.carlson@carlsoncoaching.com>
To: Tom Revere <trevere@usa.lmncorp.com>
Subject: Welcome and Getting Started!

Dear Tom,

I am looking forward to beginning our work together in November.

Attached you'll find:
1. An overview of Roles & Responsibilities for our work together
2. A New Client Intake Form
3. A Client-Coach Agreement

Prior to our first meeting, please review the Roles & Responsibilities Overview, noting any questions you have, and complete and return the New Client Intake Form and the Client-Coach Agreement to me.

Please let me know what works best for you for our first meeting. You can schedule with me using this link. I am excited to get started on our work together!

Thanks,
Andie

2-3 OVERVIEW OF ROLES AND RESPONSIBILITIES

We often share an overview of Roles & Responsibilities to prompt questions and support a conversation about how the client, coach, and sponsor will all work together during the engagement. We customize this overview to reflect the engagement. In this example the HR business partner (HRBP) is playing a supportive role.

COACH CONSIDERATION: Sometimes HR plays a supportive and valuable role in an engagement, and in other instances HR is not involved at all. Edit your Roles & Responsibilities Overview to reflect the roles in your engagement.

Roles & Responsibilities During a Coaching Engagement

During the coaching engagement, each person involved plays an active role, guided by the responsibilities outlined below.

Role	Responsibilities
Client	• Interview and select coach
	• Be accountable for your own development: commit to coaching sessions, assignments, practices, observation, and self-reflection
	• Take ownership of defining goals and drafting coaching plan, in collaboration with the coach and sponsor
	• Come prepared to sessions
	• Conduct experiments, "homework," and assessments in a timely manner
	• Provide feedback to your coach as part of tailoring the coaching process to your specific needs and context
	• Share insights and progress regularly with the sponsor
	• Seek feedback on progress from key stakeholders
Coach	• Provide coaching using an approach, tools, and materials tailored to the client, their coaching goals, and the organizational context
	• In collaboration with the client, align on engagement goals with the sponsor (and HR if appropriate)
	• Collaborate on and refine the coaching plan with the client; update as needed
	• Provide focus on the goals and a structure for achieving them throughout the engagement
	• Provide appropriate feedback and progress with the sponsor and HR while maintaining confidentiality

COACH CONSIDERATION: Typically, this might include a sense of where we are in the process and the degree of the client's and sponsor's engagement. If content (e.g., progress against goals) is to be shared, we talk with our clients directly about what to share.

Sponsor	• Provide perspective on the client's development
	• Help define the coaching goals and give input to the coaching plan
	• Provide continuous feedback and support to your client
	• Participate in progress review sessions with coach, client, and HR at midpoint and end of coaching program
HRBP	• Provide input on coaching goals and share perspective on the client's development
	• Provide organization context as needed—organizational expectations, tool/assessment, preferences/approach, etc.
	• Help resolve any issues with the coaching engagement
	• Participate in progress review sessions with the coach, client, and sponsor as needed
	• Provide support with contract and billing issues

2-4 COACH-CLIENT AGREEMENT

Note: This Coach-Client Agreement was shaped by examples coaches and organizations generously shared over the years.

A Coach-Client Agreement covers the way you and your client will work together and includes things such as the responsibilities you each have in the coaching process, agreement on scheduling and changing meetings, the role of confidentiality, and how you will stay aligned and share feedback with one another throughout the engagement. Send your client the agreement after the kickoff meeting with a request to sign and return it to you.

> COACH CONSIDERATION: It is particularly important to create an agreement between the coach and client when the SOW has been completed with the organization.

Coach-Client Agreement

Coaching is designed to create new awareness and understanding for the client, and help build new mindsets, behaviors and skills, that enhance professional development and personal growth. To achieve these objectives:

Coach's Responsibilities

- The coach will work together with the client to schedule coaching sessions and to develop a coaching plan that addresses the goals identified and agreed upon.
- The coach will, over the course of the engagement, involve the client's manager (as the sponsor) to collect feedback, and, in partnership with the client, to align on goals and share progress.
- When using an assessment, the coach will recommend ones in accordance with the organization's plans, preferences, and approach to assessments.
- The coach will work with the client to create goals and a coaching plan, including resources, potential actions, and practical strategies that will support the client in achieving their goals.
- The coach will work with the client to identify and address obstacles and patterns that get in the way of progress toward the goals.
- The coach will provide continuous reinforcement and encouragement to the client.
- The coach will work with the client to identify strategies to sustain the changes made in coaching and craft an ongoing development plan to implement after the coaching engagement.

Client's Responsibilities

- The client is responsible for actively participating in coaching sessions, including identifying mindsets, behaviors, and skills for improvement; designing experiments related to the goals; practicing new behaviors or approaches; engaging in exercises and simulations in coaching sessions; and observing progress throughout the coaching process.
- The client is responsible for their own growth, learning and participation in the coaching process by being prepared and on time for sessions and, as needed, recognizing the limits of coaching and when other services or processes may be more beneficial. The client understands that coaching is not a substitute for counseling or legal services.
- The client will give feedback to the coach, proactively or when requested, to refine the coaching approach so the coaching can best support the client and their goals.

Coaching Logistics

- Coaching sessions will be scheduled at times mutually agreed on by the client and the coach.
- The frequency of coaching sessions will be determined by mutual agreement between the client and the coach.
- All coaching sessions will take place through a mix of in-person meetings, telephone, email, video conference and other electronic communication as agreed by the client and the coach.

- To the extent possible, the client will contact the coach 48 hours before a scheduled session if a scheduling conflict arises. This does not apply to emergency or unforeseen situations. The coach will provide the same advance notice of schedule changes.
- From time to time, the client may contact the coach for an urgent situation. The coach will make their best efforts to respond to such a request in a timely manner.
- Cancelled sessions will be rescheduled by mutual agreement and according to the client's and coach's availability.

Confidentiality

Without revealing information shared in confidence, the coach will encourage and support open dialogue and sharing between the client and their manager including data, insights and learnings from the 360° and any assessments.

The coach assures that all information and communications provided by the client or the organization will be kept strictly confidential and will not be shared with anyone without express permission by the client or unless required by law as in instances of child or elder abuse, and in certain instances where there is a threat to life (suicide or homicide), or the destruction of property. The client understands that the coach may, with the client's consent, use the client's name and identifying contact information only for the purpose of meeting professional certification requirements in the field of coaching.

***

By signing this document, Andie Carlson (coach) and Tom Revere (client) agree to abide by the responsibilities outlined below during their 6-month coaching engagement, which begins in April 2023.

Signatures

Client: Tom Revere, VP of Operations, LMN International

Date: _____

Coach: Andie Carlson

Date: _____

2-5 NEW CLIENT FORM

Note: When creating client-facing forms and exercises, include spacing for clients to respond to questions in document.

New Client Form

Name
Date
Mailing Address
Phone (put * by preferred) (w)   (m)
Email address(es)
Date of Birth (MM/DD)

Spouse/Partner's Name Here (If Applicable)

Children's Names and Ages Here (If Applicable)

Place of Employment

Current Work Title and Function

Professional Fields of Study and Experience:

Please Answer the Following Questions:
1. Why coaching? Why now?
2. Past coaching experiences (have you utilized a coach in the past, and if so, how was your experience)?
3. What are the desired outcomes you are looking for from this coaching engagement?
4. What, if any, obstacles might get in the way of you reaching these outcomes?
5. Are there issues, problems, and/or crises you seem to encounter repeatedly?
6. What are your greatest personal strengths?
7. What are your greatest professional strengths?
8. What are your most significant personal and professional accomplishments?
9. How do you limit yourself?
10. How do you learn best? What kind of support do you like to get? How do you like to be challenged?
11. How can I best help you reach your goals?
12. What other information, if any, do you think it would be helpful for me to know?

> **COACH CONSIDERATION:** Some coaches use separate forms and share them at different times early in the engagement. The first (shown here) asks for basic information. The second (2-9) offers additional reflection questions. Other coaches use a single form to gather all this information.

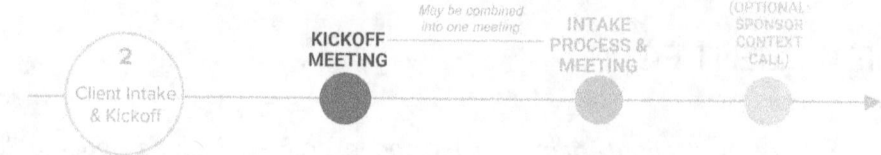

THE KICKOFF MEETING

Note: For purposes of this workbook, we present the Kickoff Meeting and the Intake Meeting as two separate meetings. If you prefer to combine these activities, you can easily integrate the tools and checklists below to match your approach.

CHECKLIST: THE KICKOFF MEETING

☐ Review notes from your previous conversations with your client and organization ahead of the kickoff conversation; make a note of questions you have not covered yet.

☐ Send a Kickoff Meeting email ahead of the session with your client (2-6), including your client-specific Next Steps list based on your earlier conversations with your client and the organization (2-7).

☐ Have your Coaching Process Overview (1-6) and Next Steps list (2-7) ready to share with your client during the session.

2-6 NEW CLIENT KICKOFF MEETING EMAIL

From: Andie Carlson <andie.carlson@carlsoncoaching.com>
To: Tom Revere <trevere@usa.lmncorp.com>
Subject: Our Coaching Kickoff

Hi Tom-

I'm looking forward to our kickoff call tomorrow. There's nothing you need to do ahead of it—I'm sharing this agenda and the attached information so we can refer to it when we talk.

Agenda
- Reconnect: how you have been since we last spoke, your current thoughts on coaching
- Walk through the attached Coaching Process Overview and explore any questions you have
- Talk about your work style, what that means for our work together, how best to schedule, etc.
- Agree on Next Steps (see attachment)
- Discuss any important dates we need to schedule around (important meetings, vacations, etc.)
- Agree on the timing of our next meeting and the 360° assessment process

Warmly,
Andie

As you draft the email, consider the following:
- How long has it been since you last connected with your client and what updates will be useful?
- What discussions have you already had with your client about the coaching process and roles and responsibilities? With this context in mind, what is needed to gain clarity and agreement with your client on the coaching process, roles, and responsibilities?
- What is your client's style (e.g., structured or free-flowing)? We structure our communications so that they are easy for our client to read (e.g., we provide more data for detail-oriented clients).
- What does your calendar look like for the next 4–6 weeks? Based on this, what adjustments do you need to make to your typical Next Steps list before you send it?

2-7 NEXT STEPS LIST

There are a number of things for both client and coach to do when starting an engagement. We share an overview of these activities with the client during our kickoff so that we are aligned on next steps. To make this easy, we maintain a Next Steps template for new clients and tailor it for each client as appropriate.

The Next Steps list below is for an engagement in which we've not yet spoken with the manager; the client will do an Enneagram assessment as part of intake, and we've agreed during contracting that we'll do an interview-based coaching 360° assessment.

Getting Started

1	Tom	Please send a note introducing me to your manager; I'll schedule time with her to talk about process, roles, and the context for coaching.

Self-Reflection

2	Andie	Send a self-reflection exercise and set of questions that will help you prepare for our coaching intake conversation.
3	Tom	Ahead of doing the self-reflection work, review any relevant performance reviews and/or any assessments (e.g., MBTI, HBDI, Social Styles, etc.) that you think would be helpful; please send me anything you'd like me to review as a means of getting to know you.
4	Tom	Complete the self-reflection exercises and send to me in advance of our first coaching meeting.
5	Andie	Review all materials in advance of our first coaching meeting.

Assessment Process

6	Tom	Complete the Enneagram assessment. I will provide you with a link to the assessment via email.
7	Andie	Send Tom a 360° email with an overview of the process, a spreadsheet to capture the list of 360° contributors, and a draft email he can send to invite contributors to participate.
8	Tom	Ask your Executive Assistant (EA) to support the interview scheduling. I will provide him with my availability.

Meetings

9	Both	Have our first coaching meeting where we get to know each other better, review your self-reflections, and further explore your early thinking about the goals for coaching.

THE INTAKE PROCESS AND MEETING

These activities may be integrated into the Kickoff Meeting, based on what you find works best for you and your clients.

CHECKLIST: POST-KICKOFF ACTIVITIES

☐ Send your client self-reflection questions and exercises to complete ahead of the meeting (2-8 and 2-9).

☐ Schedule time in your calendar just before the Intake conversation to prepare and get present for the conversation.

☐ Review your client's materials if you've asked them to send responses ahead of the Intake conversation.

TOOLS, TEMPLATES, AND EXAMPLES

2-8 INTAKE CONVERSATION PREPARATION EMAIL (OPTION 1)

From: Andie Carlson <andie.carlson@carlsoncoaching.com>
To: Tom Revere <trevere@usa.lmncorp.com>
Subject: Intake Conversation Preparation

Hi Tom-

I'm looking forward to our first coaching conversation next week. This email includes the self-reflection exercises that will form the basis of our conversation. Prior to sitting down to do this self-reflection, it's helpful to review past performance evaluations and any leadership assessments (e.g., DiSC, Strengths Finders, Enneagram, MBTI, etc.) you've found impactful.

1. LifeLine Exercise. This is a long-term view of your life—the high points and low points of satisfaction/fulfillment, and what meaning you make of it.

> **COACH CONSIDERATION:** Lifeline exercises are common coach tools, and you likely already have one in your tool kit. If not, you can find examples on the internet—some great starting points include Research in Practice's Supervisor Program and Commitment. uk.com

> **COACH CONSIDERATION:** Reflection questions and/or exercises shift your client into a coaching mindset and prepare them for a rich intake call.

2. Reflection Questions. After doing the lifeline, please take some time to reflect on and capture your responses to these questions. You can pick and choose which you'd like to respond to. Some may be juicy areas for you, others less so. Write as much or as little as you'd like. Note: The questions about coaching are included to help shape our work, though keep in mind that this early thinking will evolve as we explore the 360° and our work continues to unfold.

Additionally, I'd welcome seeing any performance reviews or assessments you think will provide useful context for our work together.

Please send your responses at least one day ahead of our meeting next week. I look forward to exploring your reflections with you as well as your overall experience of doing this reflective work. Let me know if you have any questions.

Warmly,
Andie

2-9 CLIENT INTAKE REFLECTION QUESTIONS

Here we've shared questions we often send to a new client as an attachment to the intake conversation preparation email. We've also provided options you may choose to use instead of or in addition to the ones in the example provided.

Welcome to the start of your coaching. Please take time to pause and reflect on what's brought you here and where you're wanting to go. I'd appreciate seeing your response to these questions ahead of our meeting, and I look forward to exploring these with you.

Self-Reflection Questions
1. How do you define a successful life?
2. What is working in your life?
3. Under what circumstances are you happiest?
4. What are your values? How well are you living them at the moment?
5. How does your early life experience shape who you are today and inform how you show up in the world?

6. If your life were a book, what would be the title? What's the next chapter about?
7. What are your strengths?
8. What (if anything) is getting in the way of the next level of your success or evolution?
9. In past situations when you've felt stuck or in a rut, what brings you to action?
10. How do you think about self-care? What things are important to you being your best self?

Questions About Coaching

1. If you have worked with a coach in the past, what learnings can we apply to our work together?
2. Early thinking: How would you currently articulate your goals for coaching? What's the priority (1 low to 10 high) you'd place on each? How much energy do you have for achieving each (1 low to 10 high)? For each goal, what would success look like? Sound like? Feel like?

ADDITIONAL SELF-REFLECTION QUESTIONS TO OFFER YOUR CLIENT

- What's your big dream or vision for your life? What is the role of work in that dream?
- What do you stand for as a person?
- What excites you, what lights you up?
- What book, song, piece of art or location has had significant meaning in your life? How?
- What role does spirituality play in your life?
- You are at your best when ____.
- What gets you into trouble? What gets you out of trouble?
- Is your life one of your choosing? If not, which parts are being chosen for you?
- What is your favorite part of your typical day? Least favorite?
- Looking at the past six months of your life, do you like the direction your life is moving?
- On a scale of 1 to 10, 10 being high, rate the amount of stress in your life right now. What are your primary stressors?
- What lessons have you learned so far in life?

MY NOTES:

- What do you want in your life that you don't yet have?
- What is your greatest challenge?
- What inspires you?
- What do you need to change, if anything, to reach your goals?
- What would you most like to contribute to the world?

ADDITIONAL QUESTIONS ABOUT COACHING TO OFFER YOUR CLIENT

- What successes have you had in the past that motivate you to now tackle the goals that bring you to coaching?
- What are a few things you normally don't share with people that would help me, as your coach, understand and best support you?
- What ideas do you have about how we can best work together?
- Is there anything else that would be helpful for me to know so I can best support your development?

OPTIONAL: SPONSOR CONTEXT CALL

Most, though not all, successful coaching engagements are supported by an active and involved client sponsor. If your client's sponsor participated in the initial inquiry discussion and contracting, you have likely accomplished the goals below. However, if you have not yet spoken to the client sponsor, ask the client to make the introduction and suggest a context call in order to:

- Build a relationship with your client's sponsor
- Clarify the roles you'll each play in supporting your client through the coaching engagement and how confidentiality will be maintained
- Understand the ecosystem in which your client is operating, and the business results your client is expected to deliver during the course of the coaching, and
- Hear about the sponsor's wishes for your client's development.

CHECKLIST: OPTIONAL: SPONSOR CONTEXT CALL

☐ Send an email (2-10) ahead of the scheduled call that includes an agenda, Coaching Process Overview (1-6), and the overview of Coaching Roles & Responsibilities (2-3).

☐ Schedule time in your calendar just before the call to prepare and get present for the conversation.

☐ During or after the call, capture agreements about how you'll work together and insights about the organizational and client context. Keep these with your client file to refer to as needed.

2-10 SPONSOR CONTEXT CALL INVITATION EMAIL

From: Andie Carlson <andie.carlson@carlsoncoaching.com>
To: Sydney Sharpe <ssharpe@usa.lmncorp.com>
Subject: Request to Schedule Time re: Tom Revere Coaching Engagement

Hi Sydney-

I look forward to partnering with you as we support Tom's transition and growth in his new role. I'd like to schedule a 30-min call so I can hear your perspective on the context for Tom's coaching and discuss the coaching process along with our respective roles.

If you have an assistant who supports scheduling, please share this email with them and they can be in touch with me. If you'd rather schedule directly, please feel free to offer me times that work for you, or you can schedule with me using this link .

Many thanks,
Andie

STICKY SITUATIONS THAT CAN OCCUR DURING CLIENT INTAKE AND KICKOFF

STICKY SITUATION	WHAT TO DO
You feel pressure to start the engagement without a signed SOW.	Remind the individual managing the SOW process that you cannot begin coaching without a signed SOW.
	Communicate to your client that you are waiting for a signed SOW to begin the engagement.
	You can maintain connection and momentum with your client by scheduling the initial meetings and sending pre-work such as an intake form and reflection questions.

You skipped aspects of intake and kickoff because your client needed to jump right into coaching but are now feeling the impact of missing information and relationship building.

Send an intake form to your client prior to the intake meeting. Completing this form helps your client enter into the intake process intentionally with a coaching mindset.

If you still find yourself in this situation, consider "calling a time-out" or "pressing the pause" button and let the client know that you would like to start the next session with a mini-intake.

WAYS TO AVOID FUTURE STICKY SITUATIONS DURING INTAKE AND KICKOFF

STICKY SITUATION	HOW TO PREVENT
Your client is surprised by or is resisting elements of the coaching process (e.g., 360 assessment, alignment meetings with sponsor)	See Chapter 1: Sticky Situations, How to Prevent
Your client is difficult to schedule or regularly cancels coaching meetings.	Review and gain clear agreement on the coaching process, expectations, and roles and responsibilities during the kickoff process.
Your client is unresponsive to your emails and/or calls.	
Your client expects you to set the agenda for coaching sessions.	
Your client expects advising, consulting, and/or solutions during coaching conversations.	

Many sticky situations occur because a client and/or sponsor does not fully understand the coaching process and/or the roles and responsibilities of the client, coach, and sponsor. Share your coaching process and discuss roles and responsibilities in intake and kickoff discussions to proactively manage expectations.

COACH CONSIDERATIONS: In rare instances it may be necessary to have a candid conversation, sharing your observations of the client's behavior. And in even rarer instances you may need to call into question the client's ability to commit to coaching right now and consider a pause or ending the engagement.

YOUR TURN

HOW CAN YOU BRING MORE INTENTION TO CLIENT INTAKE AND KICKOFF?
Reflect on your current practices and the materials shared here.

1. What are you currently doing well?

2. Where would you like to develop, experiment, and/or learn more?

3. I am energized to experiment in these areas:

WHAT TOOLS AND PRACTICES WILL HELP YOU STRENGTHEN THIS ASPECT OF YOUR PRACTICE?

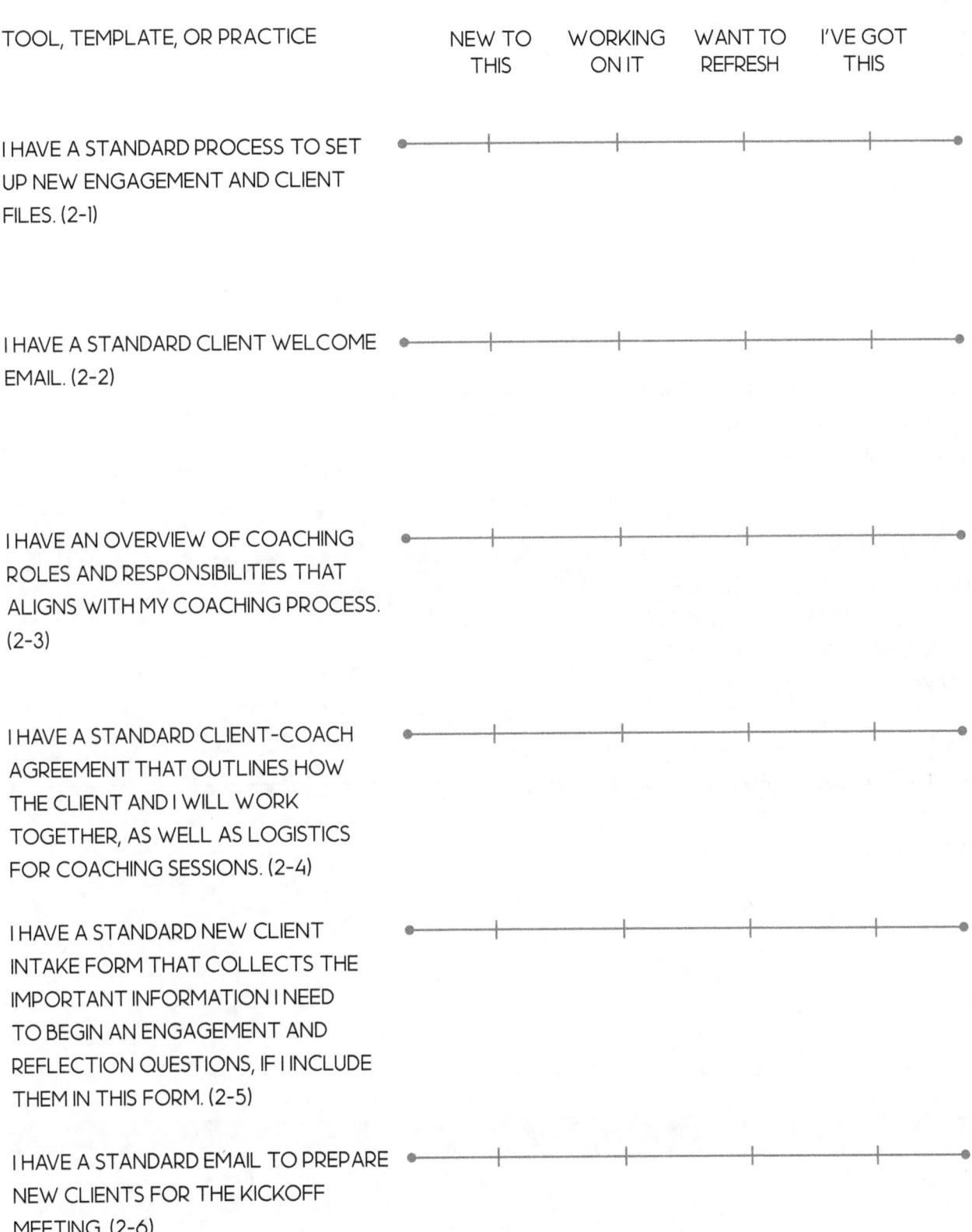

TOOL, TEMPLATE, OR PRACTICE	NEW TO THIS	WORKING ON IT	WANT TO REFRESH	I'VE GOT THIS
I HAVE A STANDARD PROCESS TO SET UP NEW ENGAGEMENT AND CLIENT FILES. (2-1)				
I HAVE A STANDARD CLIENT WELCOME EMAIL. (2-2)				
I HAVE AN OVERVIEW OF COACHING ROLES AND RESPONSIBILITIES THAT ALIGNS WITH MY COACHING PROCESS. (2-3)				
I HAVE A STANDARD CLIENT-COACH AGREEMENT THAT OUTLINES HOW THE CLIENT AND I WILL WORK TOGETHER, AS WELL AS LOGISTICS FOR COACHING SESSIONS. (2-4)				
I HAVE A STANDARD NEW CLIENT INTAKE FORM THAT COLLECTS THE IMPORTANT INFORMATION I NEED TO BEGIN AN ENGAGEMENT AND REFLECTION QUESTIONS, IF I INCLUDE THEM IN THIS FORM. (2-5)				
I HAVE A STANDARD EMAIL TO PREPARE NEW CLIENTS FOR THE KICKOFF MEETING. (2-6)				

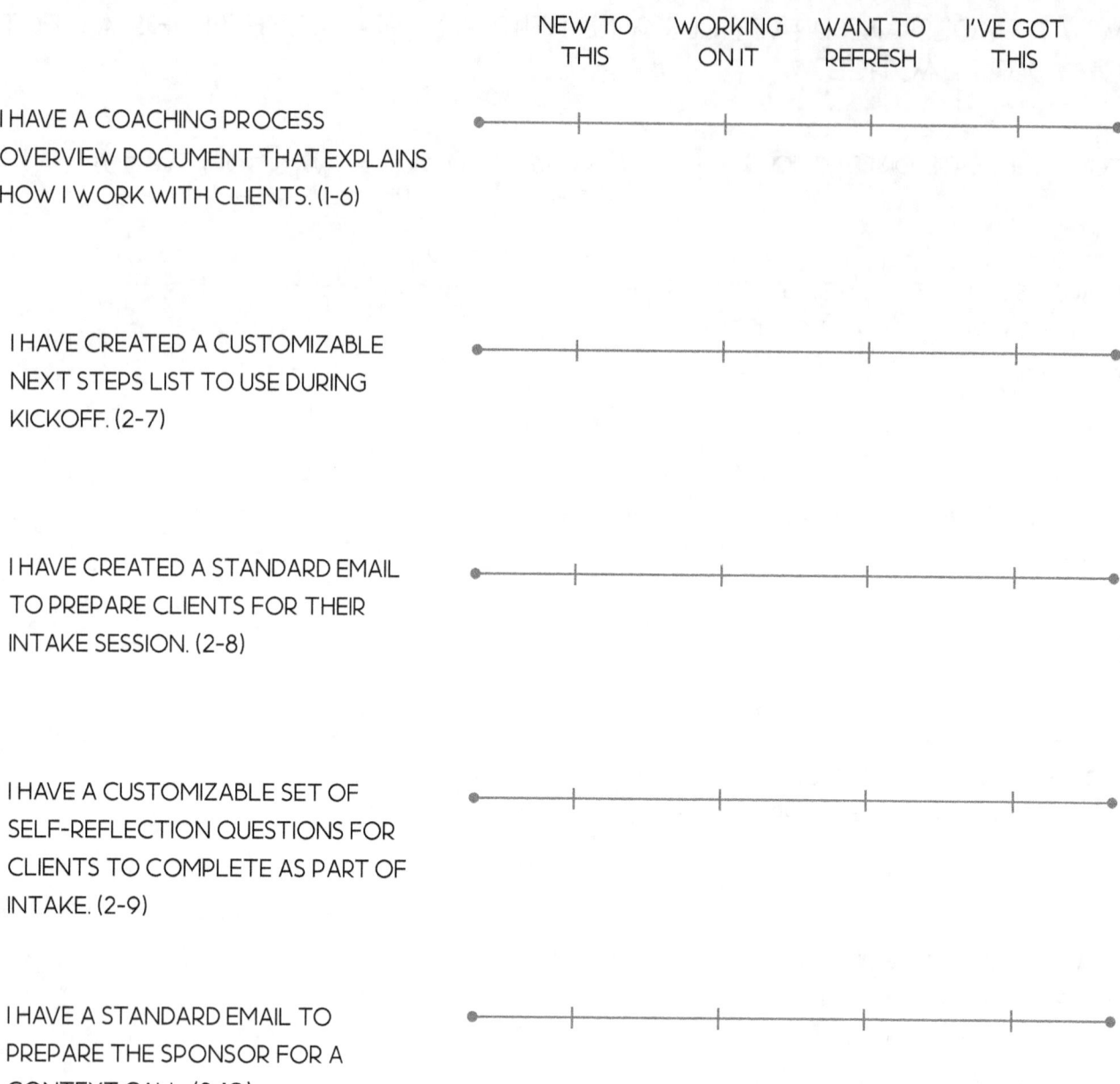

	NEW TO THIS	WORKING ON IT	WANT TO REFRESH	I'VE GOT THIS
I HAVE A COACHING PROCESS OVERVIEW DOCUMENT THAT EXPLAINS HOW I WORK WITH CLIENTS. (1-6)				
I HAVE CREATED A CUSTOMIZABLE NEXT STEPS LIST TO USE DURING KICKOFF. (2-7)				
I HAVE CREATED A STANDARD EMAIL TO PREPARE CLIENTS FOR THEIR INTAKE SESSION. (2-8)				
I HAVE A CUSTOMIZABLE SET OF SELF-REFLECTION QUESTIONS FOR CLIENTS TO COMPLETE AS PART OF INTAKE. (2-9)				
I HAVE A STANDARD EMAIL TO PREPARE THE SPONSOR FOR A CONTEXT CALL. (2-10)				

CREATE YOUR PLAN

NOTES			
TIMING			
NEXT STEPS			
TOOL OR APPROACH			

PHASE II

ESTABLISHING THE THROUGH LINE

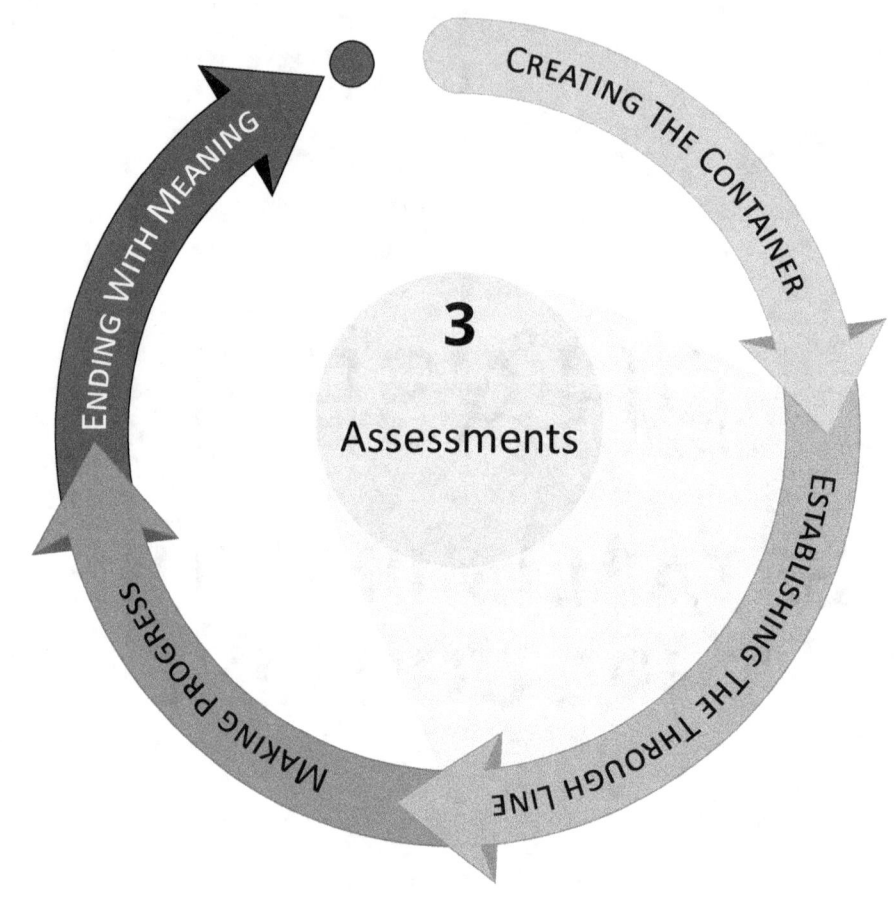

CHAPTER 3

BUILDING AWARENESS: ASSESSMENTS

I f you're familiar with *DYBC*, you'll know we cover assessments pretty thoroughly over two chapters (Chapters 3 and 3+), providing so many tools, templates, and processes that we actually drift into workbook territory! If you're new to using assessments in coaching or want to fully refresh on the topic, we encourage you to use this workbook in combination with *DYBC*. For an even deeper look at 360° assessments specifically, we recommend *Feedback Reimagined* and *Fearless Feedback* (see Resources).

Assessments are a critical element of Establishing the Through Line, which is the backbone of the coaching engagement. They offer your client the opportunity to build self-awareness, increasing their understanding of who they are, as well as an opportunity to see how they are perceived by others. For our purposes, assessments are any process or tool that identifies and describes a person's strengths, characteristics, opportunities for growth, or other unique aspects. By more clearly understanding their current state, clients are better able to envision what it will take to successfully make the changes they desire.

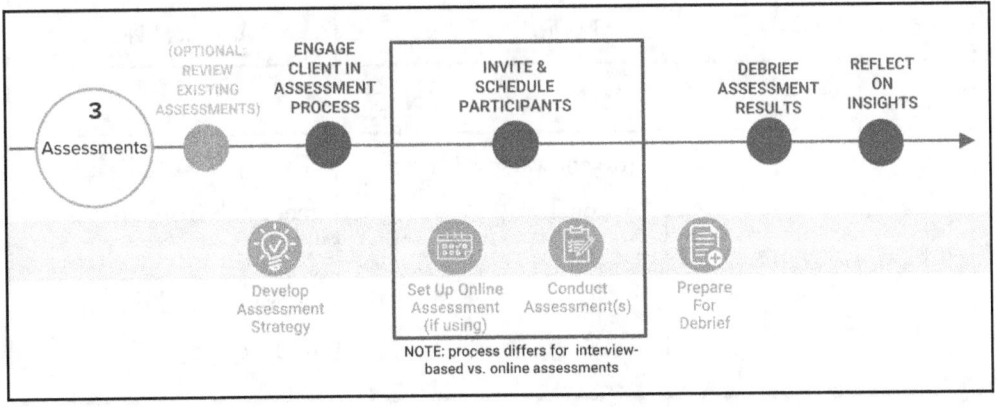

KEY OUTCOMES
ASSESSMENTS

- Increased self-awareness for your client and, in the case of a 360° assessment, greater understanding of how they are perceived by others

- Greater clarity for you of how others perceive your client, including their strengths and opportunities for development
- Actionable feedback and resulting client insights that are important inputs to the coaching goals and plan

OVERVIEW: COACHING ASSESSMENTS BY CATEGORY

To help make sense of the many types of assessments available and simplify this discussion, we have organized the world of coaching assessments into three categories:

- 360° assessments (e.g., 1:1 interview-based, online surveys such as Leadership Circle Profile, or a hybrid of the two)
- Self-Assessments (e.g., MBTI, Enneagram-iEQ9, Strengthsfinder)
- Specialist (e.g., EQ in Action, Be Well Lead Well Pulse)

To bring depth to the checklists and tools in this chapter, we've created a table that captures assessments within these categories. This table does not reflect the full nature of assessments used in coaching; rather it offers a starting point to provoke thinking as you develop an assessment strategy for your client.

 This is for illustrative purposes only, explaining why and when we use the assessment. For a detailed discussion of how to select and when to use different types of assessments, see *DYBC* Chapter 3.

CATEGORY	TYPE/EXAMPLES	APPLICATION
360° ASSESSMENTS		
1:1 Interview-Based	Interviews conducted by coach	To provide qualitative feedback from the organization on a client's strengths and development opportunities
Online	• The Leadership Circle Profile • Benchmarks® 360°	To provide quantitative and qualitative feedback from the organization on a client's strengths and development opportunities

SELF-ASSESSMENTS		
Personality and Preferences	• DiSC • HBDI • Insights Discovery • MBTI • Social Styles	To provide insight on a particular aspect of a client's working or communication style May be useful when a client is challenged by communicating or working with colleagues who operate differently
Strengths, Values, Motivators	• Enneagram • Gallup Strengthsfinder • Hogan Assessments • VIA Character Strengths Survey • Personal Values Assessment	To support a client's interest in deeper self-understanding, strengths, motivations, derailers
SPECIALIST		
Wellness / Self-Care	• Be Well, Lead Well • The Energy Audit	To offer insight into how to expand leadership capacity through a wellness lens
Emotional Intelligence	• EQ In Action Profile • EQ-i 2.0, aka Baron EQ-i • ESCI	To help a client understand their emotional impact on others and recognize and manage emotions intentionally
Progress Assessment	• Interviews • Online survey	To assess an organization's perspective of client progress and support development of the Ongoing Development Plan

COACH CONSIDERATION: While you are completing your client's 360° assessment, they will be working on articulating their core values and creating their leadership vision. They should complete this work prior to their assessment debrief so that it is not influenced by the feedback they receive.

THE ASSESSMENT PROCESS

We now dive into the nuts and bolts of the assessment process. This discussion follows the process illustration at the beginning of this chapter, and uses a 360° Assessment as the example. You will see that the majority of the steps are consistent for either an interview-based or an online assessment. However, the process does vary in the segment "Prepare, Invite and Schedule Participants." To capture these differences clearly, we offer two different tracks for this segment of the process, one for Interview-Based 360° Assessments and one for Online 360° Assessments.

Note: As most self-assessments (e.g., DiSC, Hogan) today are conducted online, we suggest you use the approach presented for online assessments, omitting the instruction to select and invite other participants.

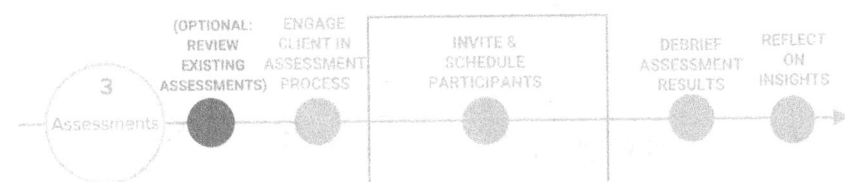

OPTIONAL: REVIEW EXISTING ASSESSMENTS

You may learn that your client was assessed prior to the start of your engagement. If this assessment was completed within the past year and the context remains the same (e.g., same role, same organization), you may want to consider using that information to support ongoing work. And, in some cases, the organization may require you to use data from a recently completed assessment.

CHECKLIST: OPTIONAL: REVIEW EXISTING ASSESSMENTS

☐ Request existing assessments from your client and ask for their take on what they found useful from the assessments and what they have tried or implemented as a result of the assessments.

☐ Review any existing assessments provided by your client.

☐ Capture themes from your review to support your assessment strategy and spark your curiosity.

DEVELOP ASSESSMENT STRATEGY

During your early conversations (e.g., initial inquiry, sponsor context, client intake) you will develop an understanding of how your client and their organization view assessments, as well as things such as organizational preferences, what assessment results are available, and your client's stance toward assessment. You will find this useful background as you begin to develop the assessment strategy.

MY NOTES:

CHECKLIST: DEVELOP ASSESSMENT STRATEGY

☐ Consider what you have learned about your client, their organization, and objectives for the engagement during early conversations, as well as timing and desired outcomes (3-1).

☐ Determine what assessments to use for this particular client situation and explain your approach to your client.

TOOLS, TEMPLATES, AND EXAMPLES

3-1 QUESTIONS TO DEVELOP AN ASSESSMENT STRATEGY

- What are the objectives for the assessment strategy? This will depend on the context, organization, and possibly your client's own awareness.
- What assessment results already exist and how can they inform the through line?
- What type of information is needed to help increase your client's self-awareness? External perspective from others? Insight into self, such as motivations, thinking style, communication style?
- What assessments meet the needs of this particular client and situation?
- What timing would be in service of the coaching:
  - What assessment is needed early in the engagement to inform the coaching goals and plan?
  - What might be useful later in the engagement to create additional insight, or a different lens to look through?
  - At what point should you do any additional assessments while ensuring you have enough time to pull through key insights before the engagement wraps up?

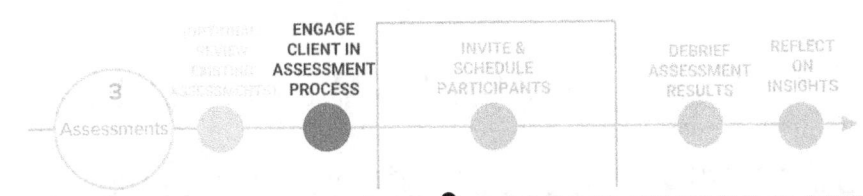

ENGAGE CLIENT IN THE 360° ASSESSMENT PROCESS*

CHECKLIST: ENGAGE CLIENT IN THE 360°
ASSESSMENT PROCESS

☐ Begin by reviewing the assessment strategy with your client, including objectives, process, timing, confidentiality for all stakeholder feedback, and your client's role in the process.

☐ Have a clear, process-oriented discussion (3-2a and 3-2b) with your client that includes the following:

  ☐ Discuss considerations for selecting the colleagues they would like to participate in the 360° (3-3).

  ☐ Share the 360° Participant Tracker (3-4) with your client to capture the list and useful content information, and remind your client to review their completed list with their sponsor before finalizing it.

☐ After your client has completed the list of participants, review the list together.

☐ Confirm that their sponsor has signed off on the list of participants your client has created.

Most self-assessments are conducted online, so we suggest you use the approach suggested for online 360° assessments, omitting the step to select and invite other participants.

TOOLS, TEMPLATES, AND EXAMPLES

3-2a INTERVIEW-BASED 360° PROCESS OVERVIEW

Interview-Based 360° Process

As we have discussed, a 360° assessment is an important element of a leader's ongoing development process, as it provides data that enables you to focus on honing your strengths and identifying and addressing areas of opportunity.

We will be conducting an interview-based assessment to create a well-rounded picture of your current strengths and opportunities. Below is the process we'll follow as well as a draft email you may use to send to participants. Feel free to edit the email to make it your own.

Step		Interview-Based 360° Assessment
1	Tom	Determine whom you'd like me to interview, which should include: • Your direct manager and 2–3 other senior leaders • 3–4 direct reports • 3–4 peers • Optional: clients, vendors, or partners
2	Tom	Share a draft list with your manager or sponsor and with me via email to gain alignment. List is finalized.
3	Tom	Email those individuals requesting their participation in your 360° assessment process, with a cc to me. *I have provided you with a draft email below that you can edit to make your own.*
4	Andie	Once I receive the cc'd email to interviewees, I will schedule interviews with them directly.
5	Andie	Conduct interviews with your colleagues.
6	Andie	Analyze the interview responses, identify the key themes, and create your assessment report.
7	Both	Meet to share and debrief your assessment report.

3-2b ONLINE 360° PROCESS OVERVIEW

COACH CONSIDERATION: Although this may seem highly tactical, using overview documents to support the discussion of these processes is very helpful as the processes have so many small steps and handoffs.

Note: While the conversation about an online 360° is largely the same as an inter-view-based assessment, the steps are different and require a different process overview.

The Online 360° Process

As we have discussed, a 360° assessment is an important element of a leader's ongoing development process, as it provides data that enables you to focus on honing your strengths and identifying and addressing areas of opportunity.

We will be conducting your online assessment using the Leadership Circle Profile to provide you with both quantitative and qualitative data. Below is the process we'll follow, as well as a draft email you may use to send to participants. Feel free to edit the email to make it your own.

Step	Responsible	Online Assessment
1	Andie	Send Tom a spreadsheet to capture the information needed (e.g., name, email address, and relationship) for the colleagues you wish to participate in the assessment.
2	Tom	Complete the spreadsheet with the contact information for the colleagues you wish to participate in the assessment.
3	Tom	Share the template with your direct manager and/or sponsor and request their input. Once the list is finalized, please send it to me.
4	Andie	Once I receive your final list of participants, I will set up the assessment in the system and then alert you to send an email invitation to participants.
5	Tom	Send the email to your colleagues requesting their participation in the online assessment **with a *cc to me.*** *I have provided you with a draft email below that you can edit to make your own.*
6	Andie	Once I receive the cc'd email to participants, I launch the assessment to the participants.
7		The online assessment is open for participation (typically for two weeks).

COACH
CONSIDERATION:
A benefit of many
online 360°
assessments is the
ability to gather
quantitative data
economically. We
try to include as
many colleagues
as reasonable, but
you can also look
to the organization
and the tool itself for
guidance on how
many participants to
include.

8	Andie	Monitor participation and send reminders as needed. If necessary, I will adjust the completion date to ensure we have enough data to provide meaningful feedback before running the assessment report.
9	Andie	Run the assessment report.
10	Both	Meet to share and debrief your assessment report.

3-3 DISCUSSION GUIDE FOR SELECTING 360° CONTRIBUTORS

- The number of contributors: For an interview-based assessment, 8–12 total contributors captures a nice breadth of perspective while minimizing diminishing returns. This number might increase if the role is highly cross-functional, or your client has recently changed roles.
- Type: A good starting point is to select equal numbers of direct reports, peers, and senior leaders, then adjust for the potential coaching needs. For example, if a client expects to be working on improving collaboration across a matrixed organization, the participant list may lean toward peers.
- Perspective: Ideally, contributors have experience/exposure to your client so they can share direct observations and impact.
- Balance: Contributors should represent diversity: gender, heritage, tenure, seniority; supporters and challengers; and in some cases, both internal and external stakeholders.
- Political considerations: In some organizations and coaching contexts, it's important that key leaders be aware of, and invested in, the coaching. For example, if Tina, the CFO, has experienced your client, Paulo, VP of Audit, as lacking executive presence, it may be useful to include Tina even if she only sees Paulo in quarterly reviews.

3-4 360° PARTICIPANT TRACKING SPREADSHEET TEMPLATE

Note: The tracking spreadsheet for an online 360° is a pared-down version of the template below and typically contains each participant's name, email address, and relationship to the client.

COACH
CONSIDERATION:
If your client has
included sensitive
context information
in the spreadsheet
for your eyes
only, be sure to
remove it before
sending to the
EA for scheduling
purposes.

360 Participants Tracker
(8-12 total)

#	Name	Role/Title	Relationship to you	Best contact info	Assistant	Assistant	Context (anything to know	Interview	Interview
1									
2									
3									
4									
5									
6									
7									
...									
...									
...									
...									

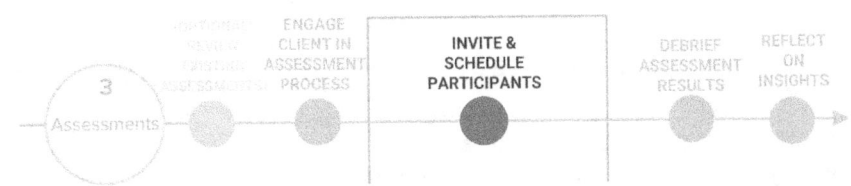

At this point, the assessment process differs for interview-based and online assessments. We illustrate these differences here using two separate tracks

TRACK 1: INTERVIEW-BASED 360° ASSESSMENTS INVITE AND SCHEDULE PARTICIPANTS

CHECKLIST: INVITE AND SCHEDULE 360° INTERVIEW PARTICIPANTS

☐ Confirm how the interviews will be scheduled and by whom.

    ☐ If working with a client's EA, talk with them about the process, share specific guidance with them, and a spreadsheet to manage the scheduling (3-4).

    ☐ If using a technology-supported approach to scheduling (e.g., Calendly), set it up appropriately before your client sends the emails inviting their participation.

☐ Share a draft email with your client that they can customize and send to participants, inviting them to participate in the 360° interviews (3-5).

☐ Once the participants have been invited to participate, scheduling can begin.

☐ Monitor the progress of the scheduling and ensure your calendar reflects all scheduled interviews; follow up as needed.

☐ Once the interview scheduling for the assessment has been completed, schedule the debrief with your client. Allow sufficient time to complete the interviews, create the assessment report materials, and prepare yourself prior to the debrief discussion.

COACH CONSIDERATION: Schedule for more time than you think will be necessary to debrief the assessment, to create a sense of spaciousness for you and your client. Debriefing is not something to be rushed through. Note that the more complicated the assessment, the more time you'll need.

3-5 INTERVIEW-BASED 360° PARTICIPANT INVITATION EMAIL

From: Tom Revere <trevere@usa.lmncorp.com>
To: Stephanie Ruke <sruke@usa.lmncorp.com>
Subject: Request for Your Participation – Coaching 360

Dear Stephanie,

As part of my professional development, I'm working with an executive coach, Andie Carlson. To help me make the most of my work and accelerate my growth, Andie is conducting confidential 360° interviews with a number of my colleagues. She will only share the results with me in aggregate, with no attribution to any single individual.

Given our work together, it's important to me to include your perspective in this process. I hope you'll be willing to schedule a 30-minute conversation with Andie in the next few weeks. She'll want to hear your thoughts on and get examples of:

- My contributions and impact

- My distinct strengths

- My opportunities to be even more effective

- Specific suggestions for leveraging strengths or being even more effective

Your honesty and candor are very much appreciated.

My EA Mark will be in touch with you to schedule the conversation. If you would prefer not to be included at this time, please let him know when he is in touch.

Thank you in advance for your contribution to this effort, and for supporting me in my professional development,

Tom

TRACK 1: INTERVIEW-BASED 360° ASSESSMENTS
CONDUCT ASSESSMENT

Note: For further insight into how to conduct an interview-based 360° assessment, please refer to:

- *DYBC*
- *Feedback Reimagined*
- *Fearless Feedback.*

CHECKLIST: PREPARE FOR AND INTERVIEW ASSESSMENT PARTICIPANTS

☐ Create the document you'll use for the data collected (3-6).

☐ Finalize the questions you'll use; you might wish to review these with your client and adjust accordingly.

☐ Consider how you want to introduce yourself and explain the purpose of the interview, and how you will use the collected data. Be prepared to address confidentiality concerns.

☐ Conduct the interviews, ensuring you capture data on how this colleague knows and works with your client, your client's strengths, and your client's opportunities. Be sure to collect specific examples and suggestions.

☐ Process your interviews as you go—this may mean rereading and editing or highlighting themes or questions the notes raise for you. Be mindful of not getting anchored to early interview themes.

COACH CONSIDERATION: Some clients have specific areas of interest they'd like the 360° results to shed light on—these may lead to specific questions you ask or areas to probe if they come up in the interviews.

COACH CONSIDERATION: Interview participants will listen closely to how you describe the reason for the coaching engagement, so it is critical to prepare a brief sentence that frames coaching in a positive manner, such as "I am working with Tom to help him be the best leader he can be."

3-6 360° INTERVIEW NOTES

There are many ways to capture interview notes. One approach is to use an Excel spreadsheet. In this example the coach has captured the name of the person being interviewed and their comment. They will later categorize and sort the comments to surface themes.

Name	Category	Comments
Joe		Very accountable person-she holds us to the highest standard. We get things done and done well but she challenges what we are doing up front to make sure its right. She is also ok when we can't get something done. As long as we are communicating. everyone knows where we stand and timelines
Joe		she has had to make a lot of hard decision but always on the best interest of the company
Joe		she gives candid feedback in a direct communication style to help me get better. I appreciate her commitment to my development
Georgia		She cares a tremendous amount. She cares about what she doing succeeding
Georgia		has a bias to action in away that is powerful. Quick to address issues with team, resourcing , when she see problems on the horizon

CHECKLIST: WRITE THE ASSESSMENT REPORT

☐ Finalize key themes and supporting evidence (3-7a and 3-7b) and write the report. This may be any format you like to work with. If the report is lengthy, consider adding an executive summary that highlights the participants involved, a list of 3–4 strengths, and 2–3 opportunities.

☐ Ensure you leave enough time to write the report, step away, and come back to review it, making any refinements necessary to ensure it captures the essential feedback from the interviews.

3-7a 360° INTERVIEW NOTES SORTING AND ORGANIZING TEMPLATE

Contributions	Emerging frameworks, hunches, themes for coaching

Strengths

Opportunities

3-7b 360° INTERVIEW NOTES CATEGORIZING AND ORGANIZING EXAMPLE

Here the coach has categorized and sorted the comments by theme

Name	Category	Comments
Joe	accountable	She is a very accountable person and she holds us to the highest standard. She is also ok when we can't get something done, as long as we are communicating along the way. Everyone knows timelines and where we stand
Christina	accountable	accountable and thoughtful
Raj	action	She is biased to action
Georgia	action	has a bias to action in away that is powerful. Quick to address issues with team, resourcing , when she see problems on the horizon
Perveen	cares	She cares a lot about her people and is extremely invested in developing her people

Here the coach has created a pivot table surfacing the density of themes and responders

Row Labels	Count of Category	Count of Comments
action	2	2
Raj	1	1
She is biased to action	1	1
Georgia	1	1
has a bias to action in away that is powerful. Quick to address issues with team, resourcing , when she see problems on the horizon	1	1
holistic	2	2
Cara	1	1
balancing everyone's needs and also being able to think critically	1	1
Robby	1	1
she has a very strong grasp on the systems pieces (technology-tech stack that supports her team and the limitations and what she can and can not do) does not come in at too high level	1	1

MY NOTES:

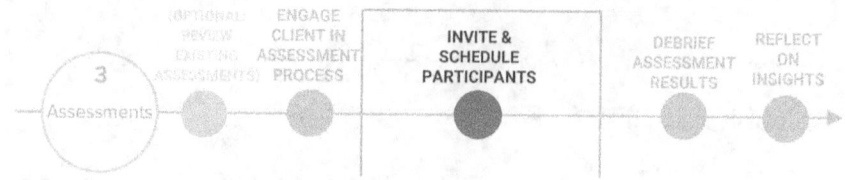

TRACK 2: ONLINE 360° ASSESSMENTS INVITE PARTICIPANTS AND SET UP ONLINE ASSESSMENT

The following assumes you regularly use an online assessment tool and are well versed in the backend system.

CHECKLIST: SET UP ONLINE 360° ASSESSMENT IN SYSTEM

❑ Set up a new assessment profile for your client in the online system you are using.

❑ Enter the required information for your client and all colleagues providing feedback.

❑ Adjust the start and end dates to match the timing you desire.

COACH CONSIDERATION: We ask our client to wait to notify their colleagues until we have set up the assessment online. This ensures you can easily and quickly launch the assessment after your client has emailed their colleagues, avoiding a lag between the two communications.

CHECKLIST: INVITE PARTICIPANTS AND LAUNCH ONLINE ASSESSMENT

❑ Notify your client that you have set up their assessment and that they can email their colleagues a request to participate. This ensures colleagues are not surprised by the assessment invitation and link that will be sent from the assessment provider once you launch the assessment.

❑ Your client invites colleagues via an email (3-8), with a cc to you.

❑ Once you receive the email (via cc), you launch the assessment to participants.

3-8 ONLINE 360° PARTICIPANT INVITATION EMAIL

From: Tom Revere <trevere@usa.lmncorp.com>
To: Raj Kohl <rkohl@usa.lmncorp.com>
Subject: Request for Your Participation – Coaching 360

Dear Raj,

Recently I began working with an executive coach as part of my commitment to my ongoing development as a leader. Part of the initial assessment process for coaching is an online 360° assessment called The Leadership Circle™, which will help me gain insight into how I lead and interact with others.

Because I value your feedback, I am asking you to participate as one of my evaluators by spending approximately 15–20 minutes to complete an online survey about me. The assessment is administered by the Leadership Circle, so I will not have access to any of the raw data. The report will consolidate all responses into an overall score and a score by category (i.e., peer, direct report...). Category scores are not broken out unless three or more responses are received to ensure anonymity.

In the next 24 hours, you will receive an email from notifications@theleadershipcircle.com with a link to the online assessment. You may want to add this email address to your "safe senders," and if you do not receive this email, please check your spam filter.

Thank you in advance for your participation, which I truly appreciate. If you have any questions about the assessment, please feel free to email or call me at any time. You may also feel free to reach out to my coach, Andie Carlson (cc'd), with any assessment-related questions.

Tom

TRACK 2: ONLINE 360° ASSESSMENTS
CONDUCT ASSESSMENT

CHECKLIST: MANAGE THE ONLINE ASSESSMENT PROCESS AND CREATE REPORT

❏ Monitor the assessment as the deadline approaches, using reminders to encourage full participation.

❏ If you find that you do not have sufficient participation as you approach the deadline, move the date later and send an additional reminder.

❏ Close the assessment at the appropriate time and initiate the report creation.

We now leave the two tracks behind and return to a shared process for interview-based and online assessments.

PREPARE FOR ASSESSMENT DEBRIEF DISCUSSION

CHECKLIST: PREPARE FOR ASSESSMENT DEBRIEF DISCUSSION

☐ Schedule time to prepare yourself for the debrief using a few guiding questions (3-9).

☐ Consider your client and how they can best explore and integrate the results; allow that to guide how and when you send the results.

☐ Send your client an email ahead of the debrief that prepares them to receive the debrief (3-10).

☐ Discuss your client's values and vision, which they completed in parallel with the assessment process, before debriefing their 360° assessment data. This ensures that your client's thought process is not influenced by the assessment data.

3-9 QUESTIONS TO PREPARE A COACH FOR AN ASSESSMENT DEBRIEF

Reflect on your client and assessment results.
- What are the key themes and messages?
- How do they align with what you already know about your client?
- How will they align with your client's sense of self?
- How do you want to show up during the debrief, and how can you be intentional about that?

3-10 CLIENT EMAIL TO PREPARE THEM FOR AN ASSESSMENT DEBRIEF

From: Andie Carlson <andie.carlson@carlsoncoaching.com>
To: Tom Revere <trevere@usa.lmncorp.com>
Subject: Request for Your Participation – Coaching 360

Dear Tom,

I'm looking forward to debriefing your 360° Assessment with you and wanted to set the stage in advance.

It's been a pleasure talking with your colleagues and pulling together your 360°. The goal of it, as you know, is to confirm your strengths and identify opportunities to accelerate your leadership development so you can have an even greater impact.

Here are some things to think about ahead of the meeting:

1. We'll be reviewing a draft of your 360° assessment via Zoom. I won't send it in advance as we'll want to talk through key messages and reactions together. If you would like to take notes on a hard copy, let me know and I'll send it as we're jumping on the call together.

2. As part of getting ready for the conversation, I encourage you to think about a few questions. No need to send a written response—we'll start here tomorrow.

> · What do you want to get from the 360° debrief conversation?
>
> · What are you expecting to hear?
>
> · How are you feeling about the 360°?

Speak soon,

Andie

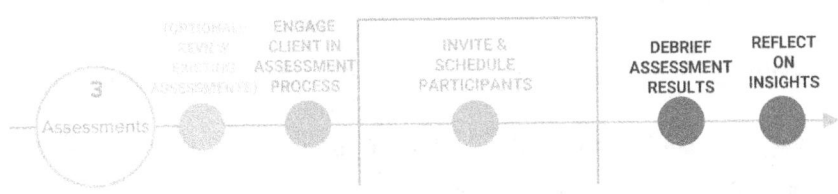

DEBRIEF RESULTS AND REFLECT ON INSIGHTS

You'll rely on your coaching skills to support the debrief conversation, as well as your knowledge and experience with the tool itself and best practices you've developed (3-11).

CHECKLIST: DEBRIEF RESULTS AND REFLECT ON INSIGHTS

☐ Share questions after the debrief to support your client's ongoing processing of the assessment results (3-12). Your client's responses and clarification questions can be discussed in a follow-up conversation, while key insights are captured to inform the coaching goals and plan.

☐ Capture your reflections and hunches about the debrief, making note of areas of high energy or intensity, any confusion, or resistance.

☐ In this or the next client conversation, discuss your client's choices in what to share with the sponsor and when to share it.

☐ You may wish to preview the sponsor alignment meeting as part of the conversation. We discuss this sponsor alignment meeting in Chapter 4 of this workbook.

TOOLS, TEMPLATES, AND EXAMPLES

3-11 BEST PRACTICES FOR ASSESSMENT DEBRIEF DISCUSSIONS

As we shared in *DYBC*, these are some practices that we consistently use in assessment debriefs:

* Recall the intention behind doing the assessment and what your client can gain from it.

MY NOTES:

- Be prepared to define jargon/terms that might not be clear to your client.

- Support your client in their own interpretation of the results—how do they make meaning from them?

- Realize that some clients may not grasp all the assessment points immediately. It can take additional reflection time, or it may not happen at all.

- Ask questions to help your client notice and process their reactions.

- Anticipate and manage your own reaction if your client becomes emotionally triggered by the assessment results.

- When your client is ready, ask them to articulate their insights from the assessment and how it informs the work they're doing in coaching.

3-12 DISCUSSION GUIDE FOR AN ASSESSMENT DEBRIEF

- What resonates from the assessment?

- What questions does it raise or where do you need clarification?

- What are you most proud of?

- What are the most important takeaways in terms of strengths?

- What are the most important takeaways in terms of opportunities?

- How do the assessment insights line up with your leadership vision and ideas about what you want to achieve through coaching?

Learn more about the complexities of debrief discussions in *DYBC* Chapters 3 and 3+

STICKY SITUATIONS THAT CAN OCCUR DURING ASSESSMENTS

STICKY SITUATION	WHAT TO DO
Your client feels over-assessed and asks to skip assessment.	Discuss your client's concern and consider if the request is reasonable: • Has your client recently been assessed using a robust tool? Can you have access to those results? • Does your client have enough data about themselves and the organizational perspective to move forward with their vision, goals, and plan in an informed way? If so, consider skipping a full assessment and explore conducting a few targeted interviews that will ensure you have the connection to stakeholders and information needed to support your client. If not, determine how to move forward to gather the information needed to inform the coaching while acknowledging your client's concern (e.g., adjust timing, consider different assessments).
Your client fears what a 360° assessment might signal to others (e.g., that they are not an effective leader).	Proactively discuss how you will position assessments positively with others in their organization. You can also share how they can position it themselves when inviting colleagues to participate (3-5 and 3-8).

The organization is concerned about rater fatigue amongst colleagues who are asked to participate in a 360° assessment.	As you create your assessment strategy, consider how the 360° assessment timing maps to the organization's talent management and business planning cycles, and adjust the timing to avoid overloading stakeholders. If you sense concern about rater fatigue as you begin the assessment process, explore the concern with your client and if necessary, the sponsor. If it's valid, discuss how to adjust sample size or timing (e.g., delay to provide the organization with a break from assessment activities). It can also be helpful to explore the differences in the types of assessments and ratings the organization has done and what you're proposing.
Your client and/or the sponsor wants more 360° participants than are included in the Statement of Work.	Discuss your client and/or sponsor's request and determine if the request is reasonable. If it's valid and the change to scope is significant, agree to an appropriate increase and provide an addendum to your SOW, adjusting fees to reflect the increase.
The assessment process is significantly delayed by scheduling issues and your client is eager to move forward.	Discuss the impact of the delay with your client and the sponsor to prevent future surprises or disappointments. During these discussions, explore options: • Can you begin coaching with the information that initiated the coaching engagement? • How else can you support your client in building awareness in the interim (e.g., other assessments)? • Does it make sense to delay the start of the engagement?

MOVES TO AVOID FUTURE STICKY SITUATIONS

STICKY SITUATION	HOW TO PREVENT
Your client's sponsor is saying you are working on the wrong things, but your client has not received feedback on the sponsor's issues.	Include your client's sponsor in the 360° assessment and weight their comments accordingly. Ask them during the interview if they've shared the feedback with your client and encourage them to do so directly. You may even offer them some coaching on how to have that conversation.

YOUR TURN

HOW CAN YOU BRING MORE INTENTION TO ASSESSMENTS?
Reflect on your current practices and the materials shared here.

1. What are you currently doing well?

2. Where would you like to develop, experiment, and/or learn more?

3. I am energized to experiment in these areas:
    a.

    b.

    c.

WHAT TOOLS AND PRACTICES WILL HELP YOU STRENGTHEN THIS ASPECT OF YOUR PRACTICE?

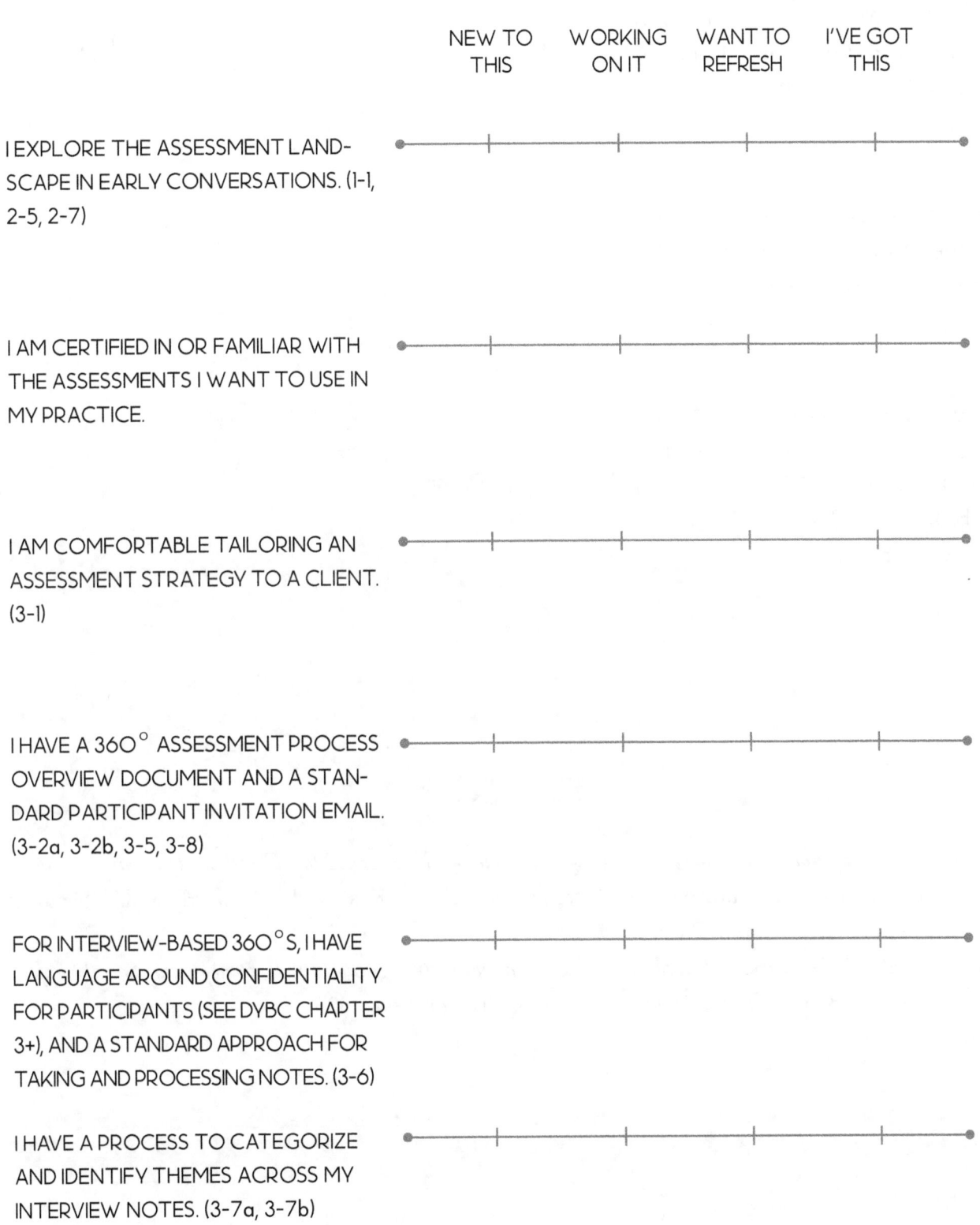

	NEW TO THIS	WORKING ON IT	WANT TO REFRESH	I'VE GOT THIS
I EXPLORE THE ASSESSMENT LANDSCAPE IN EARLY CONVERSATIONS. (1-1, 2-5, 2-7)				
I AM CERTIFIED IN OR FAMILIAR WITH THE ASSESSMENTS I WANT TO USE IN MY PRACTICE.				
I AM COMFORTABLE TAILORING AN ASSESSMENT STRATEGY TO A CLIENT. (3-1)				
I HAVE A 360° ASSESSMENT PROCESS OVERVIEW DOCUMENT AND A STANDARD PARTICIPANT INVITATION EMAIL. (3-2a, 3-2b, 3-5, 3-8)				
FOR INTERVIEW-BASED 360°S, I HAVE LANGUAGE AROUND CONFIDENTIALITY FOR PARTICIPANTS (SEE DYBC CHAPTER 3+), AND A STANDARD APPROACH FOR TAKING AND PROCESSING NOTES. (3-6)				
I HAVE A PROCESS TO CATEGORIZE AND IDENTIFY THEMES ACROSS MY INTERVIEW NOTES. (3-7a, 3-7b)				

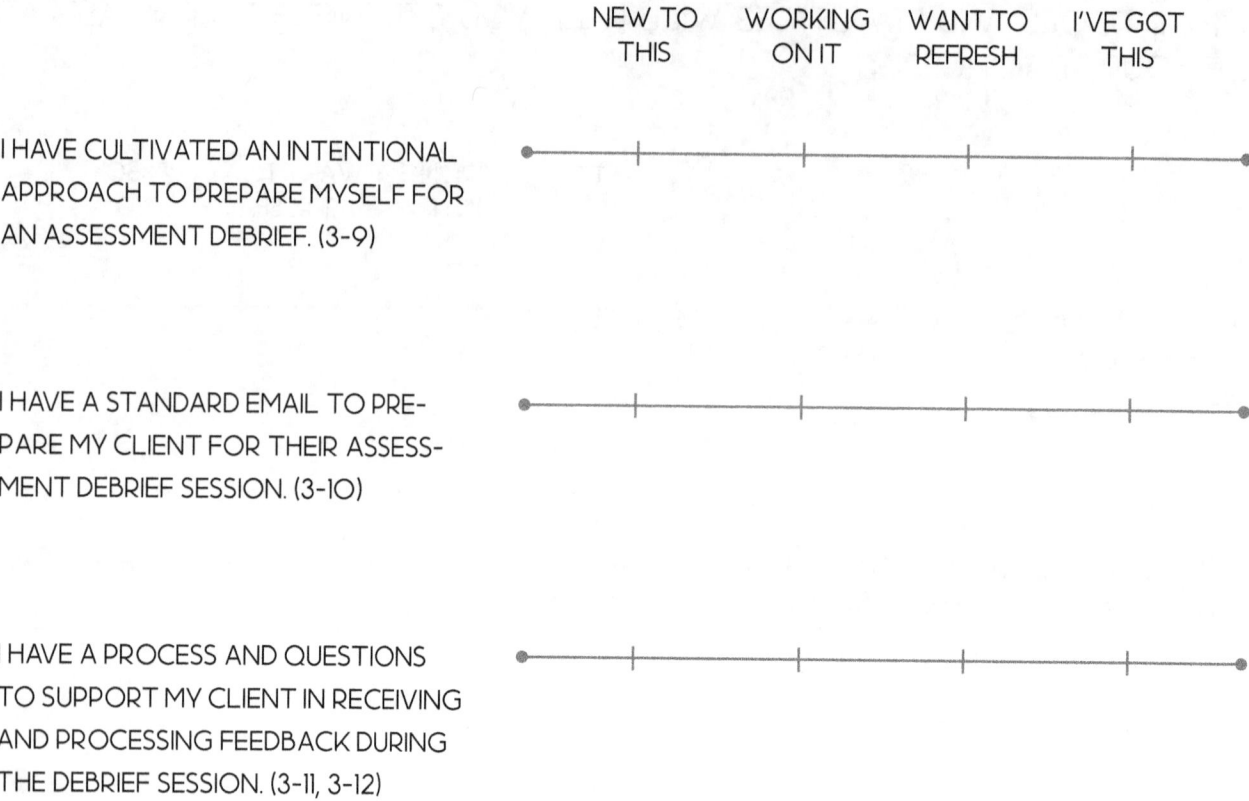

	NEW TO THIS	WORKING ON IT	WANT TO REFRESH	I'VE GOT THIS
I HAVE CULTIVATED AN INTENTIONAL APPROACH TO PREPARE MYSELF FOR AN ASSESSMENT DEBRIEF. (3-9)				
I HAVE A STANDARD EMAIL TO PREPARE MY CLIENT FOR THEIR ASSESSMENT DEBRIEF SESSION. (3-10)				
I HAVE A PROCESS AND QUESTIONS TO SUPPORT MY CLIENT IN RECEIVING AND PROCESSING FEEDBACK DURING THE DEBRIEF SESSION. (3-11, 3-12)				

RESOURCES

- *Fearless Feedback: A Guide for Coaching Leaders to See Themselves More Clearly and Galvanize Growth,* by R. Glenn, P. Handscomb, A. Kosterlitz, K. Marron, K. Ross, L. Siegworth, and T. Signorelli (Master Coach Author Press, 2019)
- *Feedback Reimagined: Transform Your Organization through Positive Psychology and Social Support,* by Peter Berridge and Jen Ostrich (Modern Wisdom Press, 2023)

CREATE YOUR PLAN

NOTES		

TIMING		

NEXT STEPS		

TOOL OR APPROACH		

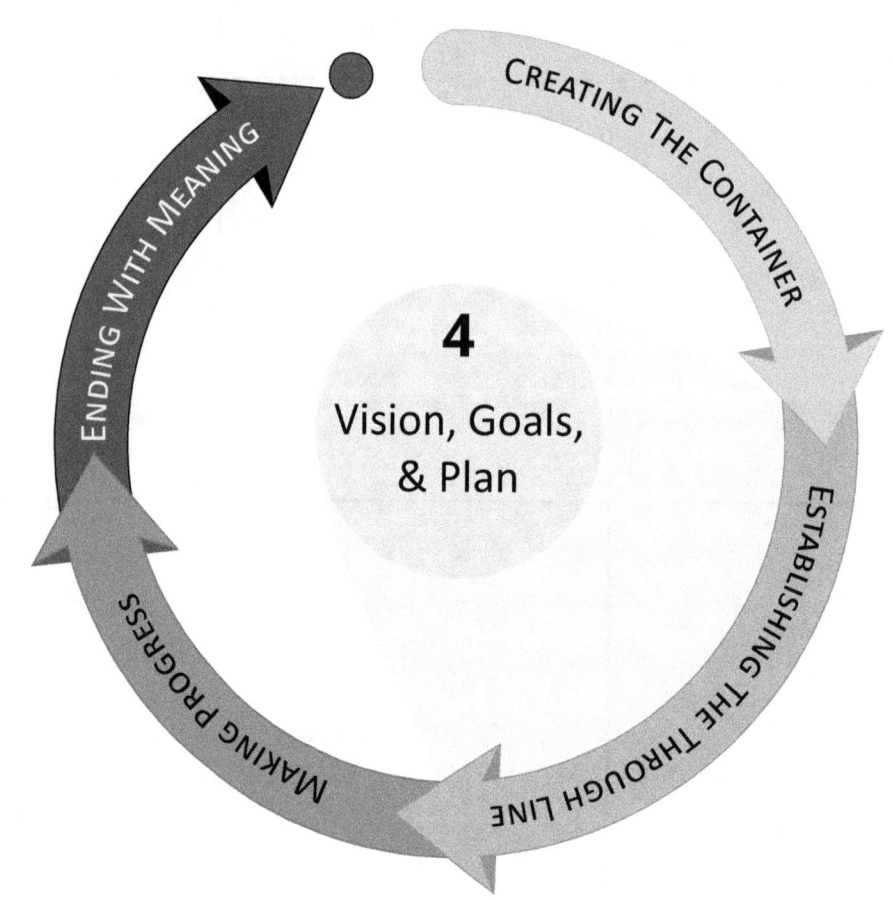

CREATING THE CONTAINER

4

Vision, Goals, & Plan

ESTABLISHING THE THROUGH LINE

MAKING PROGRESS

ENDING WITH MEANING

CHAPTER 4

CHARTING THE COURSE:
COACHING PLANS—VISION & GOAL SETTING

Early in coaching engagements, we work with clients to develop their leadership vision, which becomes the aspirational pull for the coaching goals and plan. This approach ensures that the coaching, even when initiated by a developmental need, is energizing and compelling to our clients. The insights generated through the assessment process, plus the client's leadership vision, guide the development of the client's goals and coaching plan, which are the final components of Establishing the Through Line.

While there are tools and processes that support every component of intentional engagement, we feel strongly about those that support the development of the through line. Some of the most challenging sticky situations that can arise over the course of a coaching engagement can be prevented by **Establishing the Through Line**. A solid leadership vision, along with a clear articulation of their values, encourages your client to focus on their ultimate aim of becoming their best self as a leader, and keeps them inspired and motivated to achieve it. Specific and impactful coaching goals build an achievable road map for success, and a well-developed coaching plan provides metrics to check progress and a through line for the coaching engagement. Finally, sharing the vision, goals, and plan with the client's sponsor creates alignment between the goals of the client and their organization.

Below, we dive into several ways you can support your client through this important work. As always, we encourage you to consider your approach as well as your client's unique style and adapt the offerings below accordingly.

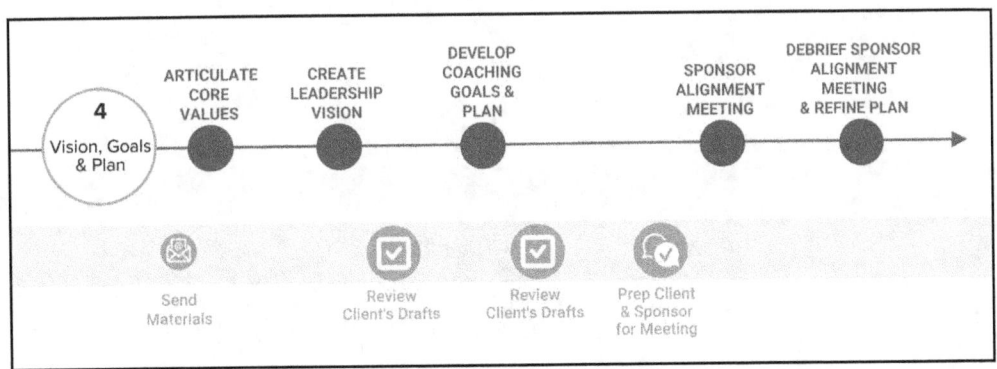

KEY OUTCOMES
COACHING PLANS — VISION AND GOAL SETTING

- Develop a compelling vision for the future to inspire coaching goals and plan
- Create meaningful coaching goals and a plan that provide a through line and focus for the client and the organization
- Enable alignment with your client and their organization on the coaching goals and plan
- Activate the sponsor to support the client's development throughout the engagement

4
Vision, Goals
& Plan

ARTICULATE
CORE
VALUES

CREATE
LEADERSHIP
VISION

DEVELOP
COACHING
GOALS &
PLAN

SPONSOR
ALIGNMENT
MEETING

DEBRIEF SPONSOR
ALIGNMENT
MEETING
& REFINE PLAN

MY NOTES:

ARTICULATE CORE VALUES

Note: Your client will complete their values and leadership vision work in parallel with the assessment process. You may discuss and support the values work and the vision work in the same conversation or in separate ones, using the checklist and tools below as appropriate for your approach.

CHECKLIST: ARTICULATE CORE VALUES

☐ If you haven't yet explored your client's communication and work preferences, do so now. For example, do they prefer to reflect and write on their own, or do they prefer to think out loud and dialogue with you in real time?

☐ Discuss the exercises that will help them articulate their values and reinforce how this work will support your client's success (4-1 through 4-7).

☐ If your client prefers to work asynchronously, email the exercises to them.

☐ Ask your client to send their draft work prior to your session so that you can review and reflect on what they have developed.

☐ Discuss the client's values before debriefing their assessment data. This ensures that the client's thought process is not influenced by the assessment data.

> **COACH CONSIDERATION:** The impact of integrating a vision with assessment data is essential to create compelling coaching goals that form the coaching plan. Your client will be developing their values and vision while you are conducting their assessment(s).

TOOLS, TEMPLATES, AND EXAMPLES

We ask our clients to consider their core values prior to creating their leadership vision, because it helps to deepen the work and ensures that they create a vision that is authentic to who they are.

Sometimes this is simply a conversation about what's important to them—what values they hold and how that applies to who they want to be as a leader, or what key experiences have made them who they are today and what values those experiences bring forward. Other times, it's useful to offer the client a list of values or even a reflective exercise to help them identify the values that are most important to them.

There are many values lists and assessments available online. We often rely on a more interactive approach, like one of the following exercises:

4-1 COACH INSTRUCTIONS FOR VALUES CARD SORT EXERCISE

Set up the exercise.
* If you are meeting with your client in person, give them a set of cards with a value on each card to review. These can be purchased online; see resources below.
* If you are meeting with your client virtually, adapt this by sending a worksheet with the cards captured in a table. Your client can then print them out and cut them into cards.

Now instruct your client to follow the steps below:
* Step 1: Sort through the deck and create three piles of cards:
    1. The 10 values that are least important to you
    2. The 10 values that are most important to you
    3. All remaining cards
* Step 2: Reflect on your top 10 important values and narrow down to your top three cards.
* Step 3: Now, reflect on a story (or stories) from your past that illustrates why these values are so important to you.
    1. What are the themes or critical threads that illuminate your selection of your top values?
    2. How do these values come through in your leadership today?
    3. Are there times when you have acted counter to these values? What was the impact?
* Step 4: How do you want to bring these values forward as you consider who you want to be as a leader in the future?
* Step 5 (optional): Review the 10 values that are least important to you. What themes or useful information can be found in this subset of cards?

Note: This exercise can be completed during a session as described above or as homework between sessions.

Here are several of the lists of values, card decks and tools available online:

- A personal values list. Gathered from multiple sources by James Clear: jamesclear.com/core-values
- Brené Brown's Dare to Lead list of values: brenebrown.com/resources/ dare-to-lead-list-of-values/
- Know Your Values Card set by Elaine Broe: leadershipcollaboratory.com/ values-cards
- Career Values Card Sort can be used online or via card deck versions: careerplanner.com/Knowdell-Career-Values-CardSort.cfm.
- Think2Perform offers an online card sort of 52 values: think2perform. com/values/#start
- The Live Your Values Deck: Sort Out, Honor, and Practice What Matters Most to You, by Lisa Congdon: lisacongdon.com
- Life Values Inventory: lifevaluesinventory.org. An online tool to help clarify personal values.
- VIA Character Strengths Survey. An online tool developed by Martin Seligman, who studies, teaches, and writes about positive psychology. The tool focuses on values in action—that is, the values you live every day vs. the values you aspire to—and then rates them for you as character strengths. This survey can be a useful starting point for a values discovery process: viacharacter.org

Below is an illustrative partial set of values we send to clients digitally when working virtually. Once they're printed and cut apart, the client can use them for a sorting exercise.

Authenticity	Fame	Peace
Achievement	Friendship	Pleasure
Adventure	Fun	Popularity

4-2 COACH INSTRUCTIONS FOR FRIENDS AND FAMILY CORE VALUES INQUIRY

Invite your client to interview 3–4 people who know them deeply, to find out what values those people see or experience as important to your client. Your client may find it useful to have a list of values (see above) to prompt the discussion.

Have your client take notes, and identify the common themes as well as their reaction to them (what resonates? what surprises?). Some possible prompts for the discussion include:

- How would you describe my impact on others? Can you tell me about a time or two when I've had a really positive effect on you or others around me?
- Based on your experience of me, what are the things you believe are important to me or that I value highly?
- How do you experience me when I'm operating as my best self?

4-3 CLIENT CORE VALUES EXPLORATION EXERCISE: HIGH POINTS REVIEW

Consider several high points in your life. For each, describe the high point and the role you played, recalling what happened, who was present, and what values you were honoring. Notice the similarities in values across high points and see what emerges for you.

High Point 1:

High Point 2:

High Point 3:

Now answer the following questions:
1. What similarities do you notice across each of these experiences?
2. What was the impact or benefit of this experience for you?
3. What was the impact or benefit for others?
4. What values do you notice across each of these experiences?

CREATE LEADERSHIP VISION

CHECKLIST: CREATE LEADERSHIP VISION

☐ Decide what tool you will use as you work with your client to craft their vision of the future (4-4 through 4-6).

☐ If you're using a writing exercise, email the exercise and ask your client to send their draft work prior to your session so that you can review and reflect on what they've developed.

☐ During your coaching session, support the client in drafting and refining a sentence or two that captures their future vision in a leadership vision statement (4-7).

☐ Discuss the client's vision before debriefing their assessment data. This ensures that the client's thought process is not influenced by the assessment data.

TOOLS, TEMPLATES, AND EXAMPLES

Below are several exercises designed to help your client create their leadership vision. We do not use all of these; instead, we adapt based on what will best support a particular client's process.

> COACH CONSIDERATION: Some clients will struggle with the "why" behind this exercise and will want to move right to their coaching plan. In these cases, it can be helpful to share the research which says clients who engage in future-focused exercises like this are more committed to the goals they set and achieve better outcomes (Passarelli 2015).

4-4 CLIENT VISION EXPLORATION EXERCISE: MEET YOUR FUTURE SELF (OPTION 1: CLIENT WRITING EXERCISE)

Use the questions and exercises below to help you articulate your personal leadership vision. You can answer these questions within this document or in a separate document.

Creating a vision takes time. Please do not rush through it. Consider working on this exercise in various segments over time, refining your responses as you reflect on past situations, personal feelings, and how you aspire to be as this future leader.

Step 1: Envision yourself <u>as the leader you wish to become.</u>

Step 2: Answer the questions below <u>as if 1–3 years have passed and you have successfully become the future leader you envisioned</u>:

1. What are the key values that define your leadership? How do these values shape your behavior as a leader?

2. What are your signature strengths as a leader? Remember you are answering this in the future, so you may add strengths you believe would be beneficial to develop.

3. What does the organization need from you as a leader to achieve its vision?

4. What observable behaviors are you exhibiting that are critical to the organization achieving success?

5. What actual significant impact are you making on the organization as a leader?

6. What observable behaviors are you exhibiting that cause others to want to be led by you?

7. What observable behaviors are you exhibiting that cause your counterparts to want to collaborate/partner with you?

8. What do you need to ensure you are not only leading for the best of the organization but for yourself as well (e.g., balance, boundaries, principles ...)?

9. What are the important roles and/or activities that give you energy outside of work? How do you ensure you are creating space and energy for these?

10. What is your leadership legacy? In other words, what will remain or continue as a result of your having lived, led, and worked in this role after you are no longer in it?

11. Envision yourself as the guest of honor at your retirement party. When others toast you as a leader, what moving things will be said that would make you feel warm and proud? What feelings do others describe in the stories about you? What would you most like the people listening to remember about you as a leader?

12. As you honestly consider the leader you are today, and the environment in which you live and work, what obstacles or gaps did you have to overcome to realize the future vision you've described? How will you plan, develop, and adapt to overcome these? What help will you need to do so, and from whom?

13. Now, with these questions answered, respond to this final question: "*When you envision yourself leading as the leader you will develop into, what does this look like?*" Paint a clear picture through words that describe you at the top of your game and being your best self as a leader.

4-5 COACH INSTRUCTIONS FOR CLIENT VISION EXPLORATION EXERCISE: MEET YOUR FUTURE SELF (OPTION 2: GUIDED VISUALIZATION)

Step 1: Envision yourself as the leader you wish to become.

Step 2: Imagine walking into a room and encountering your future self. You walk toward your future self and pause, noticing what you look like, how you stand, and the energy you are emitting.

Step 3: Sit down with your future self and engage in a discussion together.

1. What are you doing today? Why?
2. What gives you deep satisfaction?
3. What gives you joy today?
4. Who are the people that are most important to you?
5. How do you take care of yourself?
6. How would you describe your perfect day?

Finally, ask your future self:
1. What is important for me to know today so I can step into this future?
2. What obstacles should I look out for along the way?
3. What strengths will help move me forward?

4-6a COACH INSTRUCTIONS TO HELP A CLIENT USE METAPHORS TO ELICIT A VISION OF THE FUTURE LEADER

Using metaphor can be a powerful way to help leaders get out of their logical head and into their authentic heart.

1. Invite your client to think of a metaphor that captures their current self as a leader.
2. Ask curious questions to fully flesh out this metaphor and understand how they came to this selection.
3. Invite your client to think of a second metaphor that captures their desired future self as a leader.
4. Ask curious questions to fully flesh out this metaphor and understand how they came to this selection.
5. Explore the differences between the two metaphors, as this will likely be an input to their coaching plan.
6. Using the rich answers from the discussion, ask your client to consider their future self, and answer additional questions to help them fully capture the vision.

Examples of metaphors clients have shared include:
* A deeply rooted tree with branches and leaves stretching up and out to a new future
* An explorer scanning the horizon to see new possibilities

4-6b COACH INSTRUCTIONS TO HELP A CLIENT USE VISUAL IMAGES TO ELICIT A VISION OF THE FUTURE LEADER

If you suspect your client will struggle to create a metaphor, you may try using evocative visual images. There are many card decks available that can be used for just this purpose. One of the most well-known is the Center for Creative Leadership's Visual Explorer, which has 162 images.

To use this approach, follow the instructions above, but instead of asking your client to develop a metaphor, ask them to select a card from the deck with an image that represents their current state, and a second image that represents their future state. Then use the instructions in 4-6a to guide the discussion, beginning with question 2.

> COACH CONSIDERATION: If you work with clients virtually, you may want to create your own set of images online, using a tool such as Unsplash.

- Center for Creative Leadership Visual Explorer Card Deck: https://shop. ccl.org/usa/visual-explorer-facilitator-set-postcard-size-6in-x-4in.html.

4-7 CREATING THE LEADERSHIP VISION STATEMENT

Once the client has created a compelling vision, we guide them to capture the essence of it in a sentence or two. This statement will be the headline for your client's coaching plan. The coaching plan should support growth toward the future they are working to create.

For example, Tom's leadership vision from *DYBC* was:

"I will become a leader who articulates a compelling vision and strategy for my function and engages and develops my team so we can achieve it together."

MY NOTES:

DEVELOP COACHING GOALS AND PLAN

Once your client has completed their vision work and you have debriefed their assessment results with them, it's time to integrate the information into meaningful coaching goals and a plan to achieve them.

The coaching plan is anchored by your client's vision statement and contains 2–3 specific goals that support the achievement of their vision. These goals often stem from the insights harvested from their assessments and the self-awareness they have developed through your work together thus far.

CHECKLIST: DEVELOP COACHING GOALS AND PLAN

After the Vision Statement has been created and the Assessment Debrief (see Chapter 3) has been completed:

☐ Share the coaching plan template with the client and discuss the best way to work through it (4-8a and 4-8b). As with the vision and values exercises, this will be unique to each client based on their experience and working style.

☐ Support the client to develop their goals and plan.

☐ If your client is working on this between sessions, request that they send you a draft prior to your session so you can review their draft and offer observations and questions.

TOOLS, TEMPLATES, AND EXAMPLES

4-8a COACHING PLAN EXAMPLE (OPTION 1)

TOM'S LEADERSHIP VISION STATEMENT:

I will become a leader who articulates a compelling vision and strategy for my function and engages and develops my team so we can achieve it together.

DEVELOPMENTAL GOALS	BEHAVIORS AND ACTIONS (Things to Start or Stop Doing)	IMPACT OF ACHIEVING GOAL	SUCCESS MARKERS
This is your space to articulate the changes you want to make that will help you achieve your leadership vision and increase your effectiveness as a leader. Often a "from-to" statement.	*This is your space to define the practice and actions you will focus on to achieve your development goal.*	*This is your space to articulate why you are committing to these changes, and the intended outcome/ benefit for you, the organization, and employees.*	*This is your space to articulate the ways you will know you are progressing toward or have achieved your goal.*
From focusing on tactics and "most urgent" to working/ thinking strategically and focusing on "most important"	I will prioritize my key strategic objectives and ensure I have time to move each of them forward by blocking time on my calendar. I will manage email aggressively, delegating where possible, to ensure the right people at the right level are working issues. I will communi~~ this~~	Executing on our strategies will strengthen our business and move us to achieve our vision. My teams understand what is most important, prioritizing and making decisions through this lens, while minimizing churn and extraneous activity.	I am spending time on mission-critical work, not minutiae. Firefighting is drastically reduced. My direct reports are empowered and focused. ~~her~~

COACH CONSIDERATION: Sharing a template with explanations, indicated in italics here, supports the client in understanding what they might want to include in each section as they draft their goals and plan.

4-8b COACHING PLAN TEMPLATE (OPTION 2)

This is another structure to hold the client's vision, coaching goals, and plan.

***Your Name Here* - Coaching Vision, Goals, and Plan**
Today's Date Here

Leadership Vision: *Your Vision Here*

Goal 1: *Description of Goal Here*

- What might get in my way of achieving this goal:

- What resources and strengths are available to me:

- What are some potential actions I can take:

- How I will know I'm successful:

Goal 2: *Description of Goal Here*
- What might get in my way of achieving this goal:
-
- ...

THE SPONSOR ALIGNMENT MEETING ON COACHING GOALS AND PLAN

CHECKLIST: SPONSOR ALIGNMENT MEETING ON COACHING GOALS AND PLAN

❑ Once the client is well underway in drafting their coaching plan, send an email (4-9) to the client's sponsor to schedule time for the alignment meeting.

❑ Review the agenda (4-10) and process (4-11) for the alignment meeting with your client and prepare them to share their themes and insights from the assessment process, as well as their coaching plan.

❑ Conduct the alignment meeting with the sponsor and client.

❑ Debrief with the client and adjust the plan if necessary.

TOOLS, TEMPLATES, AND EXAMPLES

4-9 SPONSOR ALIGNMENT MEETING INVITATION EMAIL

This email may be sent by the coach or client. The example below is from the coach to the sponsor. If you believe it is best coming from the client (and it often is), provide the client with a draft copy and invite them to edit it to make it their own.

From: Andie Carlson <andie.carlson@carlsoncoaching.com>
To: Sydney Sharpe <ssharpe@usa.lmncorp.com>
Subject: Coaching Sponsor Alignment Meeting With Tom

Hello Sydney,

I hope this note finds you well.

I am happy to share that Tom and I have completed his 360° assessment and debrief and we are currently focused on completing his draft coaching plan.

We would like to find time to meet with you so that Tom can share his insights from the assessment as well as his draft coaching plan. We want to ensure that his goals and plan are directionally correct and aligned with the organization's needs.

Tom will be in touch with your EA to find a time that works well for the three of us.

Many thanks, and I look forward to connecting,
Andie

4-10 SPONSOR ALIGNMENT MEETING AGENDA

- Welcome and objectives
- Share themes and insights from Tom's assessment process
- Discuss Tom's draft coaching plan
- Invite Sydney to share her observations and feedback as well as suggestions to strengthen Tom's draft coaching plan
- Discuss any additional ideas to support Tom to achieve his vision and goals
- Agree to next steps

4-11 PROCESS FOR SPONSOR ALIGNMENT MEETING

Coach: Kicks off the meeting with a welcome and clear articulation of the purpose and desired outcome. Then suggest a meeting flow, asking the sponsor if there is anything they would like to add to the flow.

Client: Shares themes and insights they gained from the assessment process. Asks the sponsor if this aligns with their observations, and to offer any additional perspective that is helpful.

Sponsor: Shares their observations and additional perspectives and may ask additional questions to explore the insights.

Client: Shares draft coaching plan with their sponsor, beginning with their vision and moving through each coaching goal.
Asks the sponsor if this meets their expectations.

Sponsor: Provides feedback on the draft coaching plan and offers anything else they believe should be included.

Coach/Client/Sponsor: Discusses how to support the client in achieving their goals.
- How will the sponsor support the client?
- Who else can support the client?
- Are there opportunities (e.g., projects) that will give the client a lab in which to practice new approaches and behaviors?

Coach: Ensures alignment by asking the client and the sponsor to outline next steps.

Client: Closes, thanking the sponsor for providing the opportunity for coaching and for their support of the process.

STICKY SITUATIONS THAT CAN OCCUR DURING COACHING PLANS—VISION AND GOAL SETTING

STICKY SITUATION	WHAT TO DO
Your client is delaying work on their vision, goals, and/or coaching plan	Explore the source of the delay with your client: • If the delay is based on external issues (e.g., the client is overextended and is having trouble finding time to work on this), acknowledge the situation and co-create a workable path forward. • If the delay is driven by internal issues, help the client to work through the resistance where possible and co-create a workable path forward.
The client is struggling to create their vision, goals and/or coaching plan.	Explore and assess the client's comfort level, interest, and capacity to complete work between sessions. You may ask this directly in your intake form. If the client is open to work but still struggling, or is not open to homework, create time for them to work on this during a coaching session.

COACH CONSIDERATION: If you find your client is struggling with aspects of their coaching plan (e.g., metrics), provide examples. If they still struggle, work through defining one of the client's goals together.

STICKY SITUATIONS THAT CAN BE PREVENTED DURING COACHING PLANS—VISION AND GOAL SETTING

STICKY SITUATION	HOW TO PREVENT
Coaching is feeling heavy and focused on what is wrong with the client.	Support the client to create an aspirational and compelling vision and integrate this vision with assessment feedback to ensure their coaching goals and plan are future-focused. When the hard work of coaching leads the client to feel they're not making progress, revisit the client's vision. Their vision reminds them of their long-term goal and energizes them. If the vision crafted doesn't provide that inspiration, support the client in adjusting it so it is compelling and energizing for them.
Your client's sponsor is saying you are working on the wrong things, but your client has not received feedback on the sponsor's issues.	During the sponsor alignment meeting, provide the opportunity for the sponsor to share feedback on the coaching goals and confirm alignment on the goals when they are finalized.
The client feels stuck or that they're not making progress fast enough. You sense the client isn't getting traction, or is cycling without forward progress.	Use the leadership vision to support the development of a meaningful coaching plan. This process helps the client develop ownership for their future and commitment to what it will take to get there. The vision creates a pull mechanism that balances the hard work of coaching to get there. Avoid rushing the development of the coaching goals and plan. Take the time to: • Ensure the client has created goals that are meaningful and achievable. • Encourage the client to identify some short-term, achievable goals to build momentum.

MY NOTES:

The client doesn't want to collect progress feedback from anyone at the end of the coaching.

During the development of the coaching plan and/or during the sponsor alignment meeting, discuss the advantages of doing a pulse check with a handful of stakeholders near the end of the engagement, so the value is clear and the expectation is set early on.

Explore and discuss any concerns about progress feedback if and when they emerge.

RESOURCES

Resources for Articulating Core Values
- jamesclear.com/core-values
- brenebrown.com/resources/dare-to-lead-list-of-values/
- careerplanner.com/Knowdell-Career-Values-CardSort.cfm
- think2perform.com/values/#start
- leadershipcollaboratory.com/values-cards
- Lisacongdon.com
- lifevaluesinventory.org
- viacharacter.org

Resources for Creating a Leadership Vision
- lilyseto.com
- experientialtools.com/products/miniature-metaphors
- shop.ccl.org/usa/visual-explorer-facilitator-set-postcard-size-6in-x-4in.html
- unsplash.com
- Angela Passarelli, "Vision-Based Coaching: Optimizing Resources for Leader Development," *Frontiers in Psychology* 6 (2015): 412, doi.org/10.3389/fpsyg.2015.00412
- *Helping People Change*, by Richard Boyatzis, Melvin L. Smith, and Ellen Van Oosten (Harvard Business Review Press, 2019)

YOUR TURN

HOW CAN YOU BRING MORE INTENTION TO COACHING PLANS – VISION AND GOAL SETTING?

Reflect on your current practices and the materials shared here.

1. What are you currently doing well?

2. Where would you like to develop, experiment, and/or learn more?

3. I am energized to experiment in these areas:

   a.

   b.

   c.

WHAT TOOLS AND PRACTICES WILL HELP YOU STRENGTHEN THIS ASPECT OF YOUR PRACTICE?

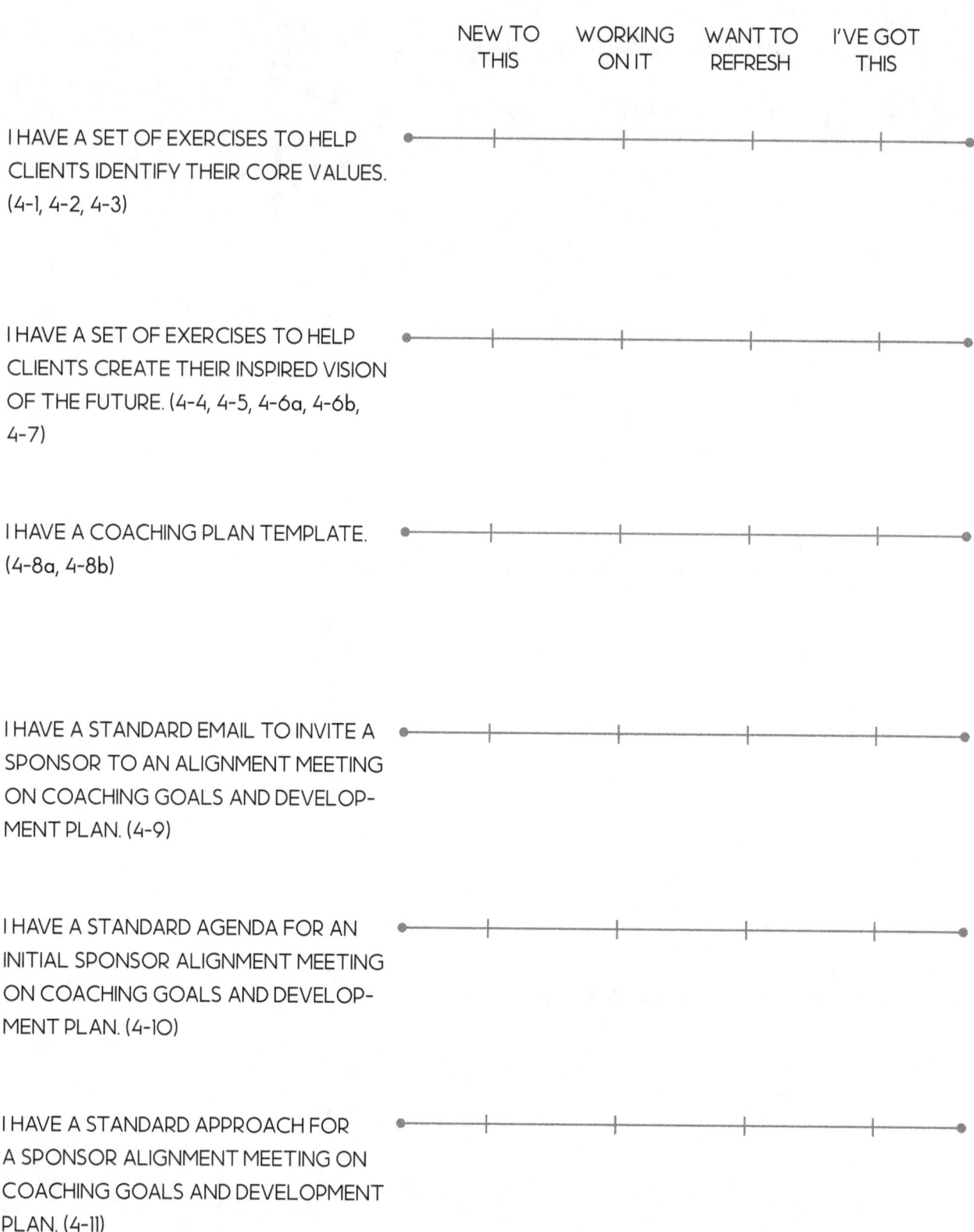

	NEW TO THIS	WORKING ON IT	WANT TO REFRESH	I'VE GOT THIS
I HAVE A SET OF EXERCISES TO HELP CLIENTS IDENTIFY THEIR CORE VALUES. (4-1, 4-2, 4-3)				
I HAVE A SET OF EXERCISES TO HELP CLIENTS CREATE THEIR INSPIRED VISION OF THE FUTURE. (4-4, 4-5, 4-6a, 4-6b, 4-7)				
I HAVE A COACHING PLAN TEMPLATE. (4-8a, 4-8b)				
I HAVE A STANDARD EMAIL TO INVITE A SPONSOR TO AN ALIGNMENT MEETING ON COACHING GOALS AND DEVELOPMENT PLAN. (4-9)				
I HAVE A STANDARD AGENDA FOR AN INITIAL SPONSOR ALIGNMENT MEETING ON COACHING GOALS AND DEVELOPMENT PLAN. (4-10)				
I HAVE A STANDARD APPROACH FOR A SPONSOR ALIGNMENT MEETING ON COACHING GOALS AND DEVELOPMENT PLAN. (4-11)				

CREATE YOUR PLAN

NOTES			
TIMING			
NEXT STEPS			
TOOL OR APPROACH			

PHASE III

MAKING PROGRESS

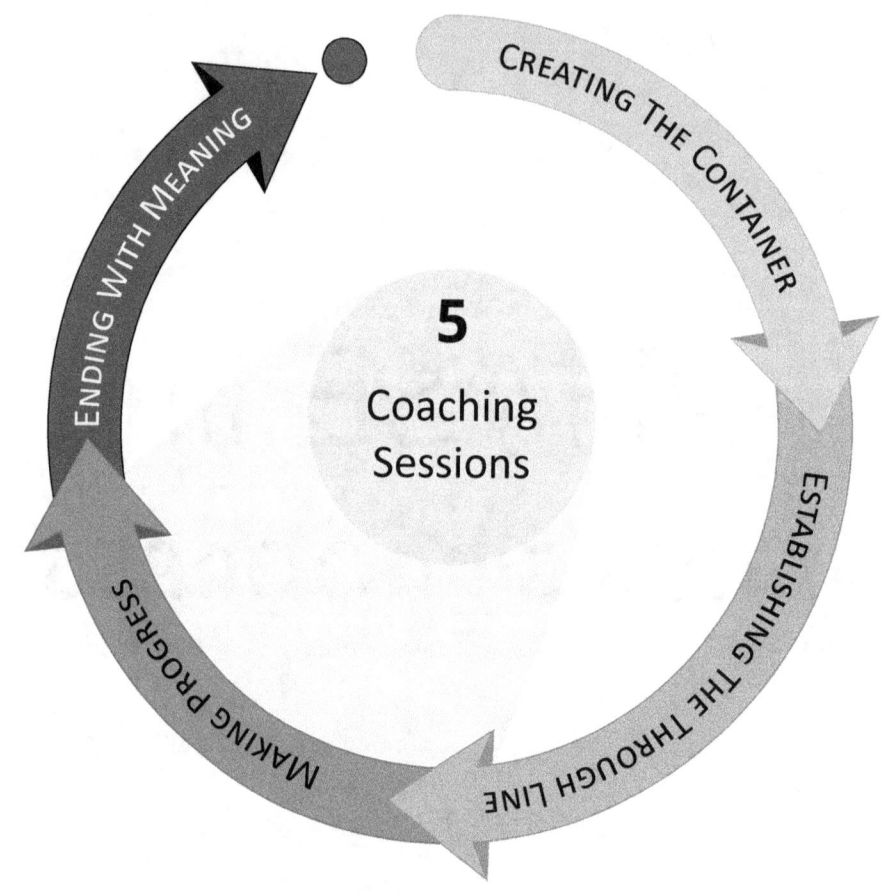

5

Coaching Sessions

CREATING THE CONTAINER

ESTABLISHING THE THROUGH LINE

MAKING PROGRESS

ENDING WITH MEANING

CHAPTER 5

BEING INTENTIONAL: THE COACHING SESSION

"Who you are is how you coach." ~ Edna Murdoch

Early in *DYBC* we share that it is not a book about how to coach or how to have a coaching conversation. And we will not tackle that here either, as there are many great programs and books that cover those topics. So if we are not discussing how to coach, what could we possibly have to say about the Coaching Session and how it supports a client Making Progress?

The Coaching Session occupies a unique space in the Intentional Engagement Framework because much of the work here is focused on being intentional about who we are as coaches, which grounds our presence and how we engage with our clients before, during, and after the session. This begins with managing our capacity so that we have sufficient time and energy to be fully present for our session. It also allows us to attend to the important work around the session (e.g., preparation and post-session documentation and reflection).

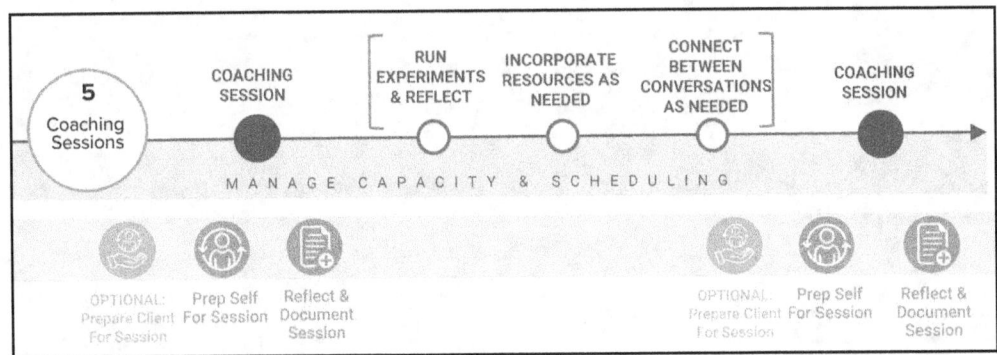

KEY OUTCOMES

- Thoughtfully manage your time and capacity to prepare for, be present to, and reflect on coaching sessions. For a detailed discussion of managing capacity, see *DYBC* Chapter 5.

MY NOTES:

- Increase awareness of patterns that might drive you to take on too many clients or start a client when the timing is not ideal.
- Mindfully enter a coaching session, maintain presence throughout, and close effectively.
- Create space for the client to reflect upon and discuss the work they are doing to make the changes they desire.
- Development as a coach through the process of post-session reflection.

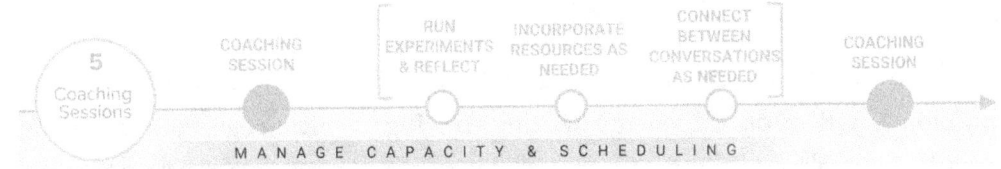

MANAGE CAPACITY & SCHEDULING

MANAGE CAPACITY AND SCHEDULING

Managing your capacity and scheduling enables you to prepare for a client session, be fully present and engaged during the session, and do the important work of reflecting afterward.

CHECKLIST: MANAGE CAPACITY AND SCHEDULING

☐ Review and update your coaching sessions tracker (5-1a) and capacity tracker (5-1b) regularly (e.g., biweekly) to ensure you are aware of your capacity.

☐ Intentionally manage new client starts to ensure your capacity is at the right level for you and your practice.

TOOLS, TEMPLATES, AND EXAMPLES

Some coaches use an online tool to schedule and track their clients, meetings, and progress such as Optify, Coaching.com, or other CRM systems. There are also online tools that primarily handle scheduling, such as Calendly.

Regardless of the tool you use, consider both the time between sessions as well as how many conversations you have capacity for in a day. We share a multitude of scheduling approaches in *DYBC* Chapter 5.

If you do not use an online tool, you can easily create your own. Following is an example of a meeting tracker (5-1a) that captures all clients at a glance. In addition to providing high-level insight into capacity, this tool ensures that we are proactively managing engagements (e.g., we are aware and able to plan for upcoming events such as mid-session alignment meetings and closings). Another approach is simply to use a sheet of paper inside each client folder to track meetings, resources shared, and key insights from each meeting.

Also following is a capacity tracker (5-1b) in which you can record the contracts and start dates, including 360° timing (a capacity limiter for most coaches), and progress check/wrap-up timing. This version is used on a whiteboard for easy adjustments.

COACH CONSIDERATION: As you receive inquiries, begin by considering the number of clients you have but also the level of difficulty and the phase of the engagement. These can impact your capacity and guide good decision-making on when it is optimal to begin new client engagements.

We update and review our tracking tools on a roughly biweekly basis, and we consciously reflect on the energy we are bringing to each engagement, paying attention to feelings of strain or overwhelm so we can be clear about where we might need to make adjustments.

5-1a SESSION TRACKER (PARTIAL VIEW)

Client Name	Client Org	Start/ Duration	Jan			Feb		
			Date	Mtg #	Topics/ Resources	Date	Mtg #	Topics/ Resources
Tom	LMN Co.	Dec, 6 months	1/7	#2	Vision	2/6	#4	Goals/ Plan re-finement
			1/22	#3	360° De-brief	2/19	----	Sponsor alignment mtg
						2/20	#5	Sponsor mtg de-brief, exec mindset
Tania	RLP Int'l	Sep, 6 months	1/15	#8	Prep for board meeting	2/1	#9	Debrief Bd Mtg, delegation
						2/16	#10	Dele-gation insights/ tweaks
					R: Cen-tering practice			
...								

5-1b CAPACITY TRACKER

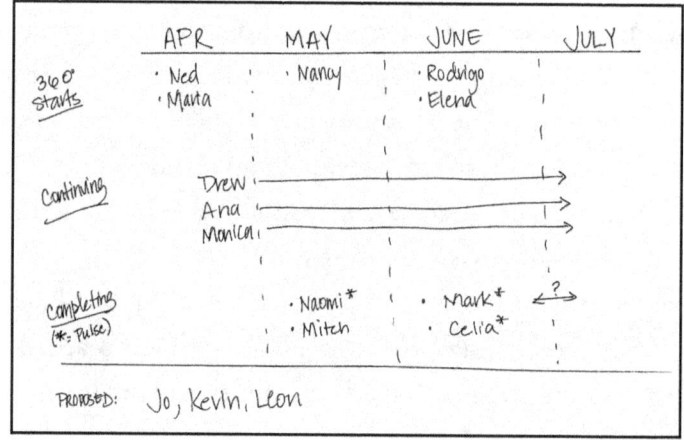

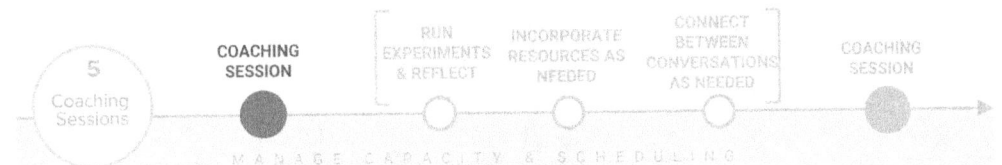

PREPARE FOR SESSION

> ### CHECKLIST: PREPARE FOR SESSION
>
> ☐ Schedule time on your calendar in advance of coaching sessions to prepare. This time may differ based on the phase of the engagement (e.g., debriefing assessments requires more preparation time).
>
> ☐ Optional: Send a pre-session preparation email to your clients (5-2).
>
> ☐ Take the time you need prior to the session to ensure you are fully present (e.g., breath work, body scan, minute of quiet). See Chapter 8 of this workbook for helpful presencing practices.

TOOLS, TEMPLATES, AND EXAMPLES

5-2 OPTIONAL: PRE-SESSION CLIENT PREPARATION EMAIL

As we researched and wrote *DYBC*, we learned that the topic of preparing clients in advance of coaching sessions is very polarizing!

If you fall into the group of coaches who do not believe in this practice, you may wish to skip right down to the next section.

For those of you who do engage in this practice or are curious about experimenting with it, approaches to preparing the client for a coaching conversation vary widely. Some coaches regularly use a prep email; some use it but not consistently, based on what's in best service to the client. Some questions to consider:

- What's the cost/benefit between client preparation time and the quality of the coaching conversation?
- Do I want the client to respond to the email ahead of the conversation, and if so, am I making time to review the response?
- Do I want to offer a consistent set of preparation cues/questions or do I want to vary it?

COACH CONSIDERATION:
If you have agreed to send your client a prep email prior to their next session, it is useful to draft it as part of your post-session documentation while the session is still fresh in your mind. Simply place the email in drafts and send when appropriate.

EMAIL EXAMPLE

From: Andie Carlson <andie.carlson@carlsoncoaching.com>
To: Tom Revere <trevere@usa.lmncorp.com>
Subject: Questions to Prepare for Coaching This Week

Hi Tom-

In preparation for our time together on Tuesday, here are a few reflection questions to consider. No need to send a response—we can discuss this on the call and it can help us shape our conversation.

1. How have you engaged your team this week in your shared strategy and goals? How is this impacting your ability to collaborate and develop your team?
2. What wins can we celebrate and what learnings can you harvest from them?
3. Where are you feeling stuck with respect to your goals? What's your hunch about how to break out of feeling stuck?
4. What's stirring for you that you want to bring forward and explore in coaching this week?

Looking forward to our conversation,
Andie

POST-SESSION DOCUMENTATION AND REFLECTION

CHECKLIST: POST-SESSION DOCUMENTATION AND REFLECTION

☐ Review the session, capturing the information that is most relevant for you and your client (5-3). You may find it helpful to protect this time on your calendar after coaching sessions.

☐ Reflect on the session, considering not only what happened, but how you showed up as a coach and how you experienced your client. Note any correlations and hunches that emerge (5-4).

TOOLS, TEMPLATES, AND EXAMPLES

5-3 POST-SESSION DOCUMENTATION

We use the term post-session documentation to denote the process of reviewing your session notes, highlighting key themes, and adding comments to augment what was captured in the session. Coaches have significantly different approaches to note-taking during the coaching session. For a detailed discussion on note-taking, see *DYBC* Chapter 5. Regardless of your approach, here are the things we capture in our post-session documentation:

- Key Themes
- Big Questions Asked
- Client Insights
- Client Takeaways
- Client Commitments Made
- Resources I Offered or Discussed

5-4 POST-SESSION REFLECTION

Post-session reflection is the term we use for pausing and considering the coaching session through an objective lens. These reflections enable us to observe patterns and gain insights about the client and ourselves. Reflections about the client can yield insights and questions we can use moving forward. Reflection about ourselves can enable us to identify strengths as well as learning edges we wish to explore further. Below we offer a collection of questions to use during post-session reflection. Select the questions that are most useful to you:

- What went well in the session? Why?
- What would I do differently if I had a "do-over"?
- What was my energy like before and after the session?
- What emotions came up for me during the session?
- What hunches did I have during the session and now?
- What did I notice about my presence?
- What did I notice about X*?
- * X = something you are working on in your coaching (e.g., presence, empathy, boundaries …)

STICKY SITUATIONS THAT CAN OCCUR DURING THE COACHING SESSION

STICKY SITUATION	WHAT TO DO
You find yourself entering coaching sessions without preparation and intentional presence.	Create time and space in your calendar to: • Prepare for coaching sessions by reviewing notes and reflections. • Use a practice of your choice to help you center and enter the engagement fully present. • Capture notes and reflections after sessions that support preparation for the next session.
You have trouble maintaining presence in coaching sessions.	Create time and space in your calendar to: • Prepare for coaching sessions, including time to center and establish presence. Reflect and explore why you are having trouble maintaining presence. • If it is driven by things in your control, consider what shifts you can make in the short and long term. • If it is related to an issue with a particular client or clients, consider how you can use this information to advance the coaching (e.g., you gently share with your client that you notice you are drifting during a conversation, and explore together).

Your coaching is suffering because you are overextended.	Consider if there's a way to change the pace of current client engagements or upcoming starts without negatively impacting the clients.
	Eliminate nonessential activities from your calendar for a few weeks. Use this freed-up time to prepare in advance of sessions and reflect afterwards.
	If clients are willing, shorten conversations by five minutes to allow both of you time to reflect and shift gears between coaching and the next commitment.
	To prevent being overextended in the future, reflect on how you became overextended and what to do differently moving forward (e.g., carefully manage engagement starts so as not to start too many at the same time).
The client feels stuck or as if they're not making progress fast enough.	See Chapter 4 Sticky Situations, How to Prevent.
	Ask if this is really true and explore why the client is feeling this way.
	Explore what they have accomplished, why they feel stuck, and/or what "fast enough" would look like.
	If you determine there is an addressable issue, revisit the client's vision and coaching plan together in your next session, and explore how the client is feeling. Together, discuss ways to help your client get "unstuck" and move forward.

You sense the client is not getting traction, or is cycling without forward progress.	If you are the one who senses an issue, ask if the traction or progress is not enough for YOU, and why. If there is an addressable issue, revisit the client's vision and coaching plan together in your next session, and explore how the client is feeling. Together, discuss ways to help your client get "unstuck" and move forward.

STICKY SITUATIONS THAT CAN BE PREVENTED DURING THE COACHING SESSION

STICKY SITUATION	HOW TO PREVENT
You don't signal the end of the engagement soon enough and your client finds it abrupt/upsetting.	See Chapters 1–2 Sticky Situations, How to Prevent Track your sessions and communicate a month before the engagement conclusion that closing is approaching.
You find yourself facing the same sticky situations again and again.	Schedule time to reflect after each coaching session. Notice when you are in a sticky situation, how you got into the situation, and how you can avoid it in the future. Consider coaching supervision to support your ability to proactively recognize and address these situations.

COACHING CONSIDERATION: No matter how intentional you are, sticky situations will still happen from time to time. Give yourself some grace and move forward with intentionality.

RESOURCES

- Calendaring systems: tools such as Calendly and Acuity are user-friendly for clients to schedule with you.
- CRM tools such as Optify, Coaching.com, and Coach Accountable offer a broader suite of offerings to help coaches manage their engagements, including calendaring.

YOUR TURN

HOW CAN YOU BRING MORE INTENTION TO THE COACHING SESSION?
Reflect on your current practices and the materials shared here.

1. What are you currently doing well?

2. Where would you like to develop, experiment, and/or learn more?

3. I am energized to experiment in these areas:
    a.

    b.

    c.

WHAT TOOLS AND PRACTICES WILL HELP YOU STRENGTHEN THIS ASPECT OF YOUR PRACTICE?

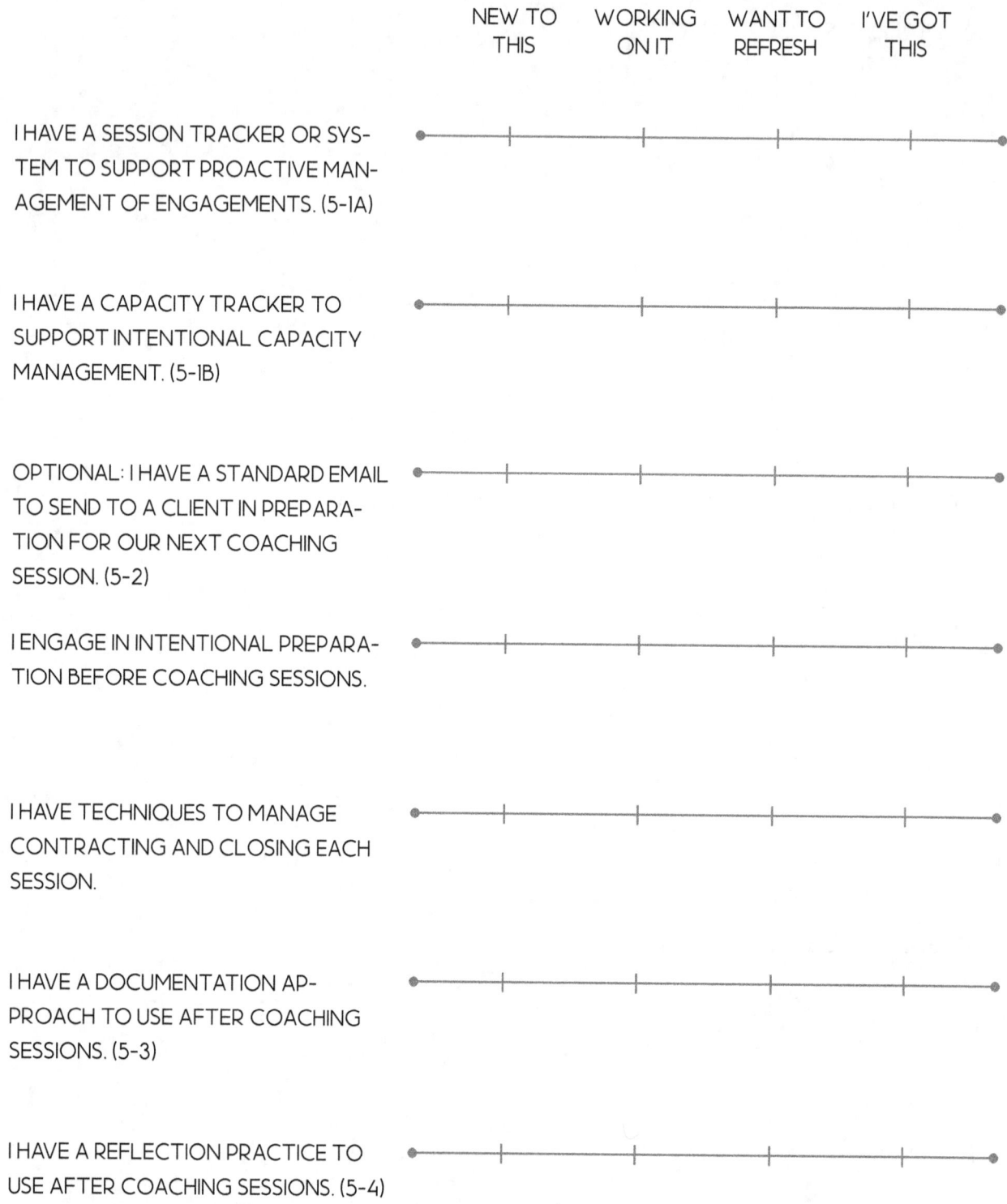

	NEW TO THIS	WORKING ON IT	WANT TO REFRESH	I'VE GOT THIS
I HAVE A SESSION TRACKER OR SYSTEM TO SUPPORT PROACTIVE MANAGEMENT OF ENGAGEMENTS. (5-1A)				
I HAVE A CAPACITY TRACKER TO SUPPORT INTENTIONAL CAPACITY MANAGEMENT. (5-1B)				
OPTIONAL: I HAVE A STANDARD EMAIL TO SEND TO A CLIENT IN PREPARATION FOR OUR NEXT COACHING SESSION. (5-2)				
I ENGAGE IN INTENTIONAL PREPARATION BEFORE COACHING SESSIONS.				
I HAVE TECHNIQUES TO MANAGE CONTRACTING AND CLOSING EACH SESSION.				
I HAVE A DOCUMENTATION APPROACH TO USE AFTER COACHING SESSIONS. (5-3)				
I HAVE A REFLECTION PRACTICE TO USE AFTER COACHING SESSIONS. (5-4)				

CREATE YOUR PLAN

NOTES			
TIMING			
NEXT STEPS			
TOOL OR APPROACH			

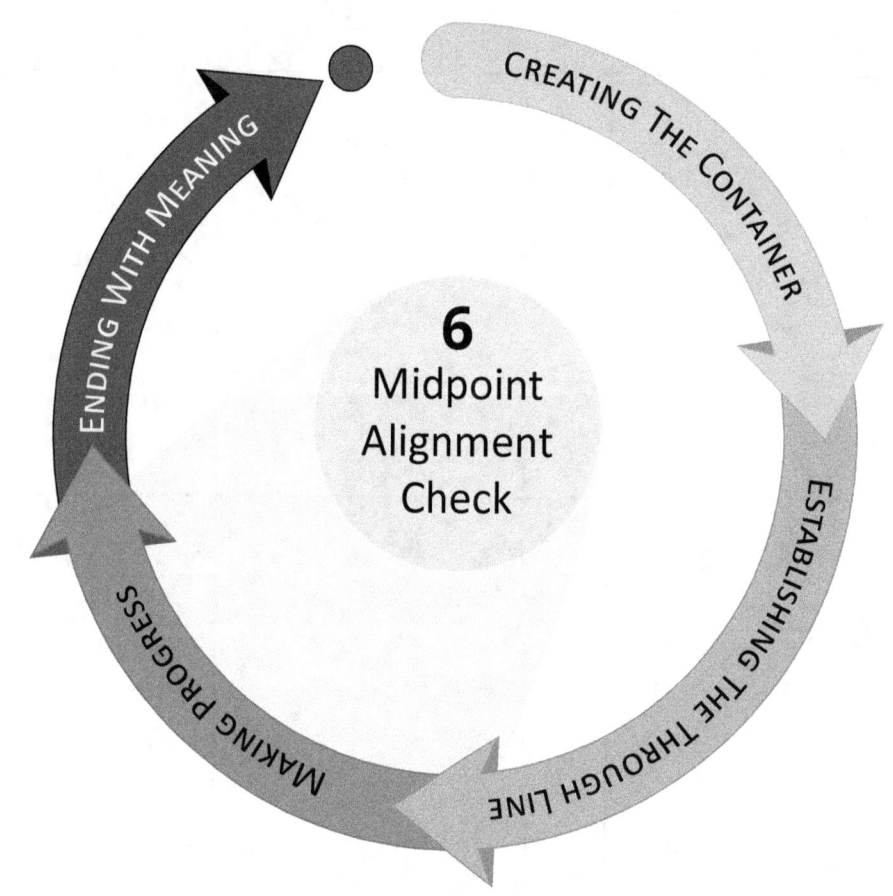

6
Midpoint
Alignment
Check

CREATING THE CONTAINER

ESTABLISHING THE THROUGH LINE

MAKING PROGRESS

ENDING WITH MEANING

CHAPTER 6

PAUSING TO CHECK CONNECTION:
MID-ENGAGEMENT ALIGNMENT

It's easy to get caught up in the energy and flow of a coaching engagement. For this reason, it's important to check for alignment, informally and formally, on the coaching engagement, relationship, process, and goals with your client throughout an engagement.

Checking for informal alignment refers to the attention you pay to your client throughout the engagement so that you notice any signs that there are issues to be addressed (e.g., your client is unresponsive to your emails and/or calls). For more information on informal alignment throughout a coaching engagement, see *DYBC* Chapter 6. When you notice these signs, check in with your client, explore what might be going on, and address it before it becomes a bigger issue. You might also find that the issue is external to the coaching relationship and/or engagement, and in that case, the client will likely be grateful to discuss what is going on.

A formal alignment discussion with your client, intentionally integrated into a coaching session at the midpoint of your engagement, serves several purposes: assessing progress, strengthening the relationship, and optimizing the coaching process. These midpoint alignment check-ins can affirm and motivate clients and may also surface helpful feedback from your client that can then be addressed. They are also an opportunity to take a step back and look at where you have been, notice if you have moved off course in any unintended ways, and agree to any adjustments. Finally, this conversation serves as preparation for a mid-engagement alignment meeting with the client and sponsor, should that be part of the engagement.

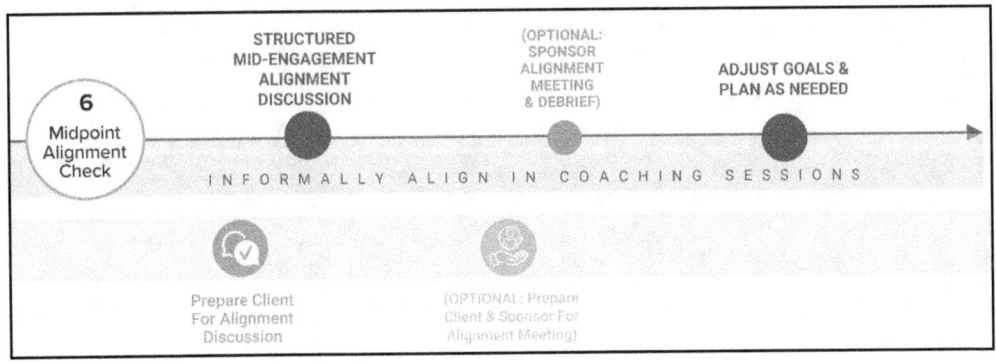

MY NOTES:

KEY OUTCOMES

- Alignment with the client on how you are working together and the progress the client is making
- Ability to address client feedback on how you are working together and adjust accordingly while still in the midst of the engagement
- Progress noticed by sponsor and the organization at the midpoint, sponsor feedback collected, and/or coaching goals refined
- Ability to address feedback from the client's sponsor on the client's goals and progress and adjust accordingly while still in the midst of the work

INFORMALLY ALIGN IN COACHING SESSIONS

INFORMALLY ALIGN IN COACHING SESSIONS
(ADDRESSING EMERGING STICKY SITUATIONS)

While we are passionate about helping coaches proactively prevent sticky situations, they still happen to everybody from time to time. By informally aligning with your client during your coaching sessions, you can stop an emerging sticky situation in its tracks. Signs that something is going on that can impact the engagement if left unchecked include:

- The client is difficult to schedule or regularly cancels coaching meetings.
- The client is unresponsive to your emails and/or calls; this can feel like the client "going dark" on you.
- The client expects you to set the agenda for coaching sessions.
- The client expects you to provide solutions.

If you notice any of these sticky situations happening during a coaching engagement, don't wait for a formal check-in to address them (unless it is scheduled for your next session). As we shared above, this is a signal to pause and have an informal alignment discussion with the client so you can learn what is happening from the client's perspective. Use it as a real-time opportunity to discuss what is happening with your client, get curious about why it's happening, and how you can solve it together.

> COACH CONSIDERATIONS:
> If you're coming across these sticky situations regularly, revisit how you're communicating and aligning on the coaching process, roles, and responsibilities in early discussions (e.g., kickoff and intake).

MY NOTES:

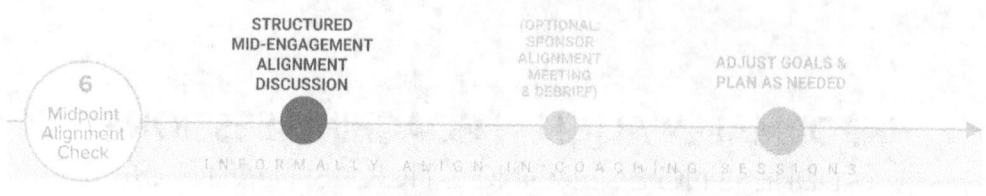

STRUCTURED MID-ENGAGEMENT ALIGNMENT DISCUSSION

CHECKLIST: PREPARE FOR CLIENT MID-ENGAGEMENT ALIGNMENT DISCUSSION

☐ Maintain your session tracker (5-1a) so you know when the midpoint is approaching.

☐ Let the client know that you would like the next coaching conversation to include a mid-alignment check-in (6-1).

☐ Share reflection questions ahead of the conversation so the client can prepare if they'd like to (6-1 and 6-2).

☐ Schedule time for yourself to prepare for the conversation.

☐ Prepare for the conversation: Review notes and reflections from the engagement to date, and identify progress, challenges, and possible improvements to the process.

CHECKLIST: FOLLOW-UP ON CLIENT MID-ENGAGEMENT ALIGNMENT DISCUSSION.

☐ Note any changes agreed to and take appropriate actions (e.g., changing timing or cadence of meetings; sending reflection questions ahead of calls, or not).

TOOLS, TEMPLATES, AND EXAMPLES

6-1 MID-ENGAGEMENT ALIGNMENT REQUEST AND PREPARATION EMAIL

From: Andie Carlson <andie.carlson@carlsoncoaching.com>
To: Tom Revere <trevere@usa.lmncorp.com>
Subject: Mid-Point Discussion As Part of Our Next Coaching Session

Hi Tom-

I'm looking forward to seeing you for our sixth session on 2/1 at 2 p.m. CT. I'd like to suggest that we take a few minutes during our meeting for a mid-engagement touchpoint. We can do this at the start or end of our session, whichever you prefer. Below are the questions I'd like to cover, and we can certainly include anything else that would be helpful from your perspective:

1. Do your coaching goals remain clear and compelling? Are there any shifts to consider?
2. From a coaching relationship and process perspective:
    a. What is going well?
    b. What shifts, if any, might be helpful to ensure you are getting the most from our time together?

Looking forward to seeing you soon,
Andie

6-2 MID-ENGAGEMENT REFLECTION QUESTIONS FOR CLIENT

Some clients and client situations call for a more robust alignment conversation at the midpoint (e.g., if the client would benefit from structured self-reflection before a conversation, or if there have been organizational changes). If you're taking this more robust approach, adapt email 6-1, using the questions that are most appropriate for your client:

MY NOTES:

For Your Coaching Goals:
1. What new insights and awareness do you have?
2. What progress are you making? What successes can you point to?
3. What are the new habits, behaviors, or skills that support your success?
4. What's been getting in your way of reaching each of your goals fully?
5. What are potential actions to take that you haven't yet explored?

About Coaching Overall:
1. Have your goals shifted since the coaching began? If so, how?
2. What direct or indirect feedback have you received? What additional feedback would be helpful and how can we best collect it?
3. Where do you want to focus as you continue?
4. What would "taking it up a notch" look, sound, and feel like?
5. What is working well in the coaching process? What is not working well in the coaching process?
6. How can your coach best support the progress you want to make?
7. What support do you need from your sponsor and/or organization to achieve your goals?

STRUCTURED
MID-ENGAGEMENT
ALIGNMENT
DISCUSSION

(OPTIONAL:
SPONSOR
ALIGNMENT
MEETING
& DEBRIEF)

ADJUST GOALS &
PLAN AS NEEDED

6
Midpoint
Alignment
Check

INFORMALLY ALIGN IN COACHING SESSIONS

OPTIONAL: SPONSOR MID-ENGAGEMENT ALIGNMENT MEETING AND DEBRIEF

This is an optional part of a coaching engagement that is particularly valuable under any of the following circumstances:

- Engagements more than six months in duration
- Engagements that include time-sensitive goals
- The client is having difficulty collecting feedback from the sponsor
- The organizational structure, the sponsor, and/or the client's responsibilities have changed mid-engagement

CHECKLIST: PREPARE FOR SPONSOR MID-ENGAGEMENT ALIGNMENT MEETING

☐ Discuss and prepare for the meeting with your client

☐ Agree with your client as to who will schedule the sponsor meeting and who will send an email about the meeting to the sponsor (6-3)

☐ Once the sponsor meeting is scheduled, also schedule a follow-up debrief conversation with your client.

CHECKLIST: DEBRIEF SPONSOR MID-ENGAGEMENT ALIGNMENT MEETING

☐ Review the conversation with your client—what did they think and feel about the conversation, and what did they learn from the discussion that they want to capture in their goals or plan?

TOOLS, TEMPLATES, AND EXAMPLES

6-3 SPONSOR MID-ENGAGEMENT ALIGNMENT MEETING AGENDA AND PREPARATION EMAIL

This email typically comes from the coach and is an informal way of preparing the sponsor for the conversation.

From: Andie Carlson <andie.carlson@carlsoncoaching.com>
To: Sydney Sharpe <ssharpe@usa.lmncorp.com>
Cc: Tom Revere <trevere@usa.lmncorp.com>
Subject: Coaching Mid-Engagement Meeting Overview

Hi Sydney (cc Tom)-

Tom and I are looking forward to our meeting with you on Tuesday morning to talk about the coaching to date. During the meeting we would like to:

- Review Tom's goals and progress toward them
- Collect your feedback on his goals and progress
- Explore any challenges in the way of success
- Refine goals, if necessary, and confirm the path forward

As a reminder, Tom is working toward becoming a more strategic leader who communicates a clear vision and develops his team to lead and execute autonomously. In support of that, he's been working on the following coaching goals:

1. From focusing on tactics and "most urgent" to working/thinking strategically and focusing on "most important"
2. ...

Please let us know if you have any questions or have anything else you want to cover,

Andie

ADJUST GOALS AND PLAN AS NEEDED

CHECKLIST: ADJUST GOALS AND PLAN AS NEEDED

☐ Support the client in revising their goals and plan as they see fit based on the coach-client alignment discussion and possibly the sponsor mid-engagement alignment meeting.

☐ Agree on how and with whom to communicate any revisions. We encourage client ownership of the goals and plan document and therefore suggest they communicate any changes.

STICKY SITUATIONS THAT CAN OCCUR DURING MID-ENGAGEMENT ALIGNMENT

STICKY SITUATION	WHAT TO DO
You're having trouble engaging the client's sponsor (e.g., can't get sponsor meetings on calendar; client isn't getting informal feedback from sponsor).	In extreme cases when a sponsor cannot be engaged, consider how to best communicate progress. For example, you may support your client to draft an email summarizing the engagement to date, and suggesting they use their upcoming 1:1 time to review the coaching plan, which they include in the email. If you have an HR contact who's been a supportive part of the coaching process, you may also consider reaching out to them to help you engage the sponsor.

MY NOTES:

Organizational changes significantly impact your client's coaching goals mid-engagement.	Have a conversation with the client and their sponsor about how to adjust the coaching goals and plan to reflect the needs of the organization and support the client's success.
A client's direct manager and/or sponsor changes roles or exits the company during the engagement, and they now have a new direct manager who does not know about the client's coaching engagement.	Have a conversation with the client and HR about how to resolve ongoing sponsorship for the remainder of the engagement. Encourage your client to tell their new manager and/or sponsor that they are engaged in coaching and request a meeting to share an overview of the process to date as well as their coaching plan. Ask your client how you two can engage the new direct manager/sponsor in the work and offer to reach out to the new direct manager and/or sponsor to introduce yourself.
The sponsor wants to have a 1:1 meeting with you and then have you deliver their message(s) to the client.	Coach the sponsor to provide the feedback to your client directly. If the sponsor is still uncomfortable having the conversation, you may offer to be present to support the conversation.
A client's sponsor says there is not enough progress.	Routinely check in with your client to ensure they are discussing their coaching with the sponsor during their 1:1's and receiving feedback. If they are not receiving sufficient feedback, be sure to schedule a mid-engagement alignment discussion.

STICKY SITUATIONS THAT CAN BE AVOIDED DURING MID-ENGAGEMENT ALIGNMENT

STICKY SITUATION	HOW TO PREVENT
You don't signal the end of the engagement soon enough and your client finds it abrupt/upsetting.	Discuss the closing process again during the mid-engagement alignment meeting with the client as well as in the sponsor alignment meeting. Address timing and remind the client and sponsor of the benefits of a strong close and their roles in the process.
You had a closing meeting with your client but not with the sponsor.	Track your sessions and, one month before the engagement conclusion, communicate that closing is approaching. Review the closing process and activities and schedule accordingly, including asking the client to proactively schedule time for the sponsor closing meeting.
The engagement ended without any closing meetings.	If you struggle with endings, resist the urge to stretch out a coaching engagement.
The client doesn't want to collect progress feedback from anyone at the end of the coaching.	Revisit the topic of progress feedback during mid-engagement alignment meetings. Throughout the engagement, ask the client about wins/successes and what feedback they're hearing from colleagues. This normalizes the role of feedback in the engagement.

YOUR TURN

HOW CAN YOU BRING MORE INTENTION TO MID-ENGAGEMENT ALIGNMENT?
Reflect on your current practices and the materials shared here.

1. What are you currently doing well?

2. Where would you like to develop, experiment, and/or learn more?

3. I am energized to experiment in these areas:
   a.

   b.

   c.

WHAT TOOLS AND PRACTICES WILL HELP YOU STRENGTHEN THIS ASPECT OF YOUR PRACTICE?

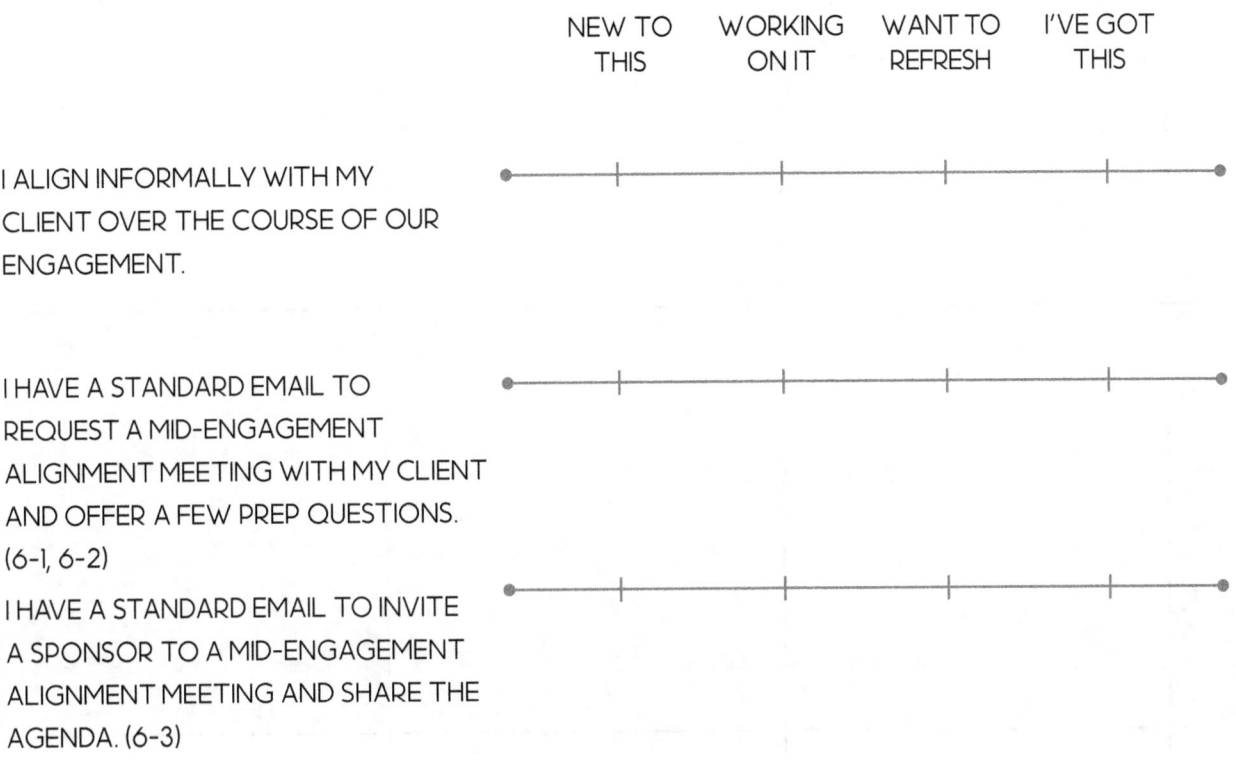

	NEW TO THIS	WORKING ON IT	WANT TO REFRESH	I'VE GOT THIS

I ALIGN INFORMALLY WITH MY CLIENT OVER THE COURSE OF OUR ENGAGEMENT.

I HAVE A STANDARD EMAIL TO REQUEST A MID-ENGAGEMENT ALIGNMENT MEETING WITH MY CLIENT AND OFFER A FEW PREP QUESTIONS. (6-1, 6-2)

I HAVE A STANDARD EMAIL TO INVITE A SPONSOR TO A MID-ENGAGEMENT ALIGNMENT MEETING AND SHARE THE AGENDA. (6-3)

CREATE YOUR PLAN

NOTES			
TIMING			
NEXT STEPS			
TOOL OR APPROACH			

PHASE IV

ENDING WITH MEANING

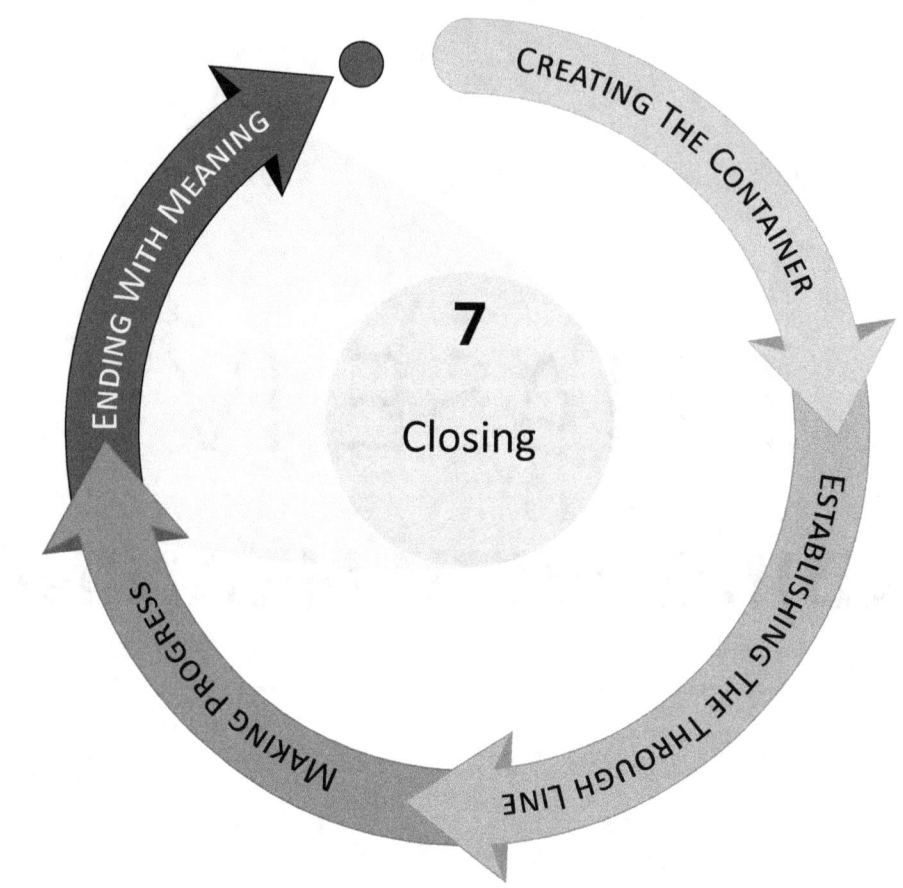

CREATING THE CONTAINER

ESTABLISHING THE THROUGH LINE

MAKING PROGRESS

ENDING WITH MEANING

7

Closing

CHAPTER 7

FINISHING STRONG:
CLOSING A COACHING ENGAGEMENT

Ending With Meaning ensures the close of an engagement is as impactful as the work that preceded it and sets the client up for ongoing success.

A strong finish allows the client and organization to recognize and celebrate progress as well as plan for future growth. While closing means an end to the engagement, it doesn't mean an end to the client's leadership vision, the learnings/practices/skills they acquired, or the relationship between coach and client.

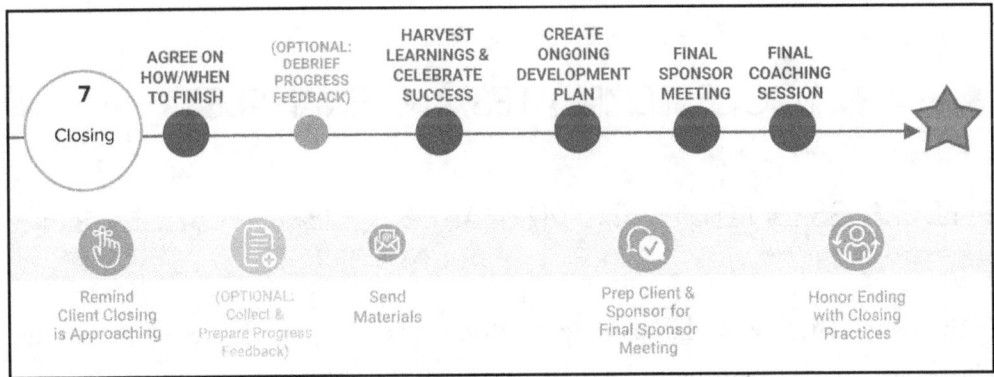

KEY OUTCOMES

- A thoughtful approach to closing for both the client and coach that honors the work done
- Encouragement and energy for the client to sustain successful change and continue their development
- The opportunity for the sponsor and the organization to recognize progress and support ongoing development
- A smooth transition out of coaching

7

Closing

AGREE ON
HOW/WHEN
TO FINISH

(OPTIONAL
DEBRIEF
PROGRESS
FEEDBACK)

HARVEST
LEARNINGS &
CELEBRATE
SUCCESS

CREATE
ONGOING
DEVELOPMENT
PLAN

FINAL
SPONSOR
MEETING

FINAL
COACHING
SESSION

REMIND CLIENT THAT CLOSING IS APPROACHING

CHECKLIST: REMIND CLIENT THAT CLOSING IS APPROACHING

❏ Maintain your session tracker so you are aware of the timing for initiating closing activities.

❏ When you're 4–6 weeks from closing, let the client know that the end is approaching and discuss the activities that create a strong close. You may choose to email your client in advance of the discussion and share the topics to be covered (7-1).

TOOLS, TEMPLATES, AND EXAMPLES

7-1 DISCUSSION GUIDE TO PREPARE A CLIENT FOR CLOSING

In this conversation with the client, we finalize the next steps and agree on the timing of closing conversations (with the sponsor, as well as the final coach-client session).

Below are the topics we cover when we're talking with the client about how to end strong. Sometimes we share these in advance if the client prefers time to think about things before discussing them:

- Timing
- Whether to collect progress feedback or not
- Types and order of conversations
  - call to review progress, build a plan for development after coaching, and prepare for sponsor conversation
  - wrap up conversation with sponsor
  - debrief of sponsor conversation and final closing
- What the client can expect to do for final reflection and planning work
- Ideas on how the client will celebrate coaching success

OPTIONAL: COLLECT, PREPARE, AND DEBRIEF PROGRESS FEEDBACK

CHECKLIST: OPTIONAL: COLLECT, PREPARE, AND DEBRIEF PROGRESS FEEDBACK

☐ If you've agreed to collect progress feedback as part of closing, decide the following with your client:

    ☐ What subset of stakeholders will be involved and who will invite them to participate (7-2)?

    ☐ How to phrase the coaching goals during the interviews.

☐ After collecting the feedback, summarize the results to share with the client (7-3a and 7-3b).

☐ Prepare to share the feedback in the same way you prepare to deliver 360° feedback (see Chapter 3).

> **COACH CONSIDERATION:** It is best practice to wait 12–18 months before doing another complete 360° assessment. However, it is helpful to do a progress check. Use an online pulse check if offered by the tool provider, or conduct your own with a handful of key stakeholders as described here.

TOOLS, TEMPLATES, AND EXAMPLES

7-2 PROGRESS ASSESSMENT PARTICIPANT INVITATION

From: Andie Carlson <andie.carlson@carlsoncoaching.com>
To: Stephanie Ruke <sruke@usa.lmncorp.com>
Subject: Request for Your Participation – Coaching Progress Check-In

Hi Stephanie-

Tom and I are at the point in our coaching work when we'd like to collect quick progress feedback from you. Tom's EA, Mark (cc'd here), will work with you or your EA to schedule a 1-to-1, 15-minute call for me to ask you about the progress you notice Tom making on his coaching goals (broadly:

becoming more strategic and setting a vision, and developing his team to execute autonomously). You may not have a line of view to be able to offer feedback on all of his goals, and that's fine.

Please also consider the broader question, "As Tom continues to grow as a leader, where would you suggest he focus his development efforts?"

Many thanks in advance,
Andie

PROGRESS FEEDBACK SUMMARY

Below are two different approaches for sharing progress feedback with your client. Both are equally impactful; experiment with which works best for how you like to work.

7-3a PROGRESS FEEDBACK SUMMARY EXAMPLE (OPTION 1)

Development Goals	Progress Observed by Colleagues	Opportunities to Continue to Develop
From focusing on tactics and "most urgent" to working/ thinking strategically and focusing on "most important"	"Tom just led us through an exercise looking into how we are investing in each area of the business. It was thoughtful and strategic." Additional Colleague Feedback	"I still notice some times when he could delegate more to me and other team members by setting a deadline and the outcome and then letting us tackle it." Additional colleague feedback
Goal 2	Colleague Feedback	Colleague Feedback
Goal 3	Colleague Feedback	Colleague Feedback

7-3b PROGRESS FEEDBACK SUMMARY TEMPLATE (OPTION 2)

Coaching Progress Feedback Summary

Date Here

Client Name and Title Here

Colleagues interviewed: Insert Names Here

Leadership Vision: Insert Leadership Vision Here

Original Goals: Insert Goals Here

Feedback by Coaching Goal

1. Insert Goal 1 Here
   - Summary statement about degree of progress observed across colleagues interviewed and consistency of responses
     - Supporting examples (if using direct quotes, be mindful of confidentiality expectations)

2. Insert Goal 2 Here
   - Summary statement about degree of progress observed across colleagues interviewed and consistency of responses
     - Supporting examples (if using direct quotes, be mindful of confidentiality expectations)

   ...

Path Forward
   - Summary statements of suggestions about how to continue to make progress, address ongoing opportunities and any potential watchouts
     - Supporting examples (if using direct quotes, be mindful of confidentiality expectations)

Words of Support
   - Specific quotes from interviews, being mindful of confidentiality expectations

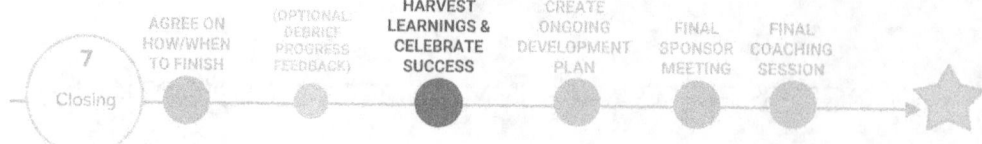

SEND MATERIALS TO HARVEST LEARNINGS AND CELEBRATE SUCCESS

CHECKLIST: SEND MATERIALS TO HARVEST LEARNINGS AND CELEBRATE SUCCESS

❑ Create a set of reflection questions appropriate for the client and the work you've done together (7-4).

❑ Send reflection questions with plenty of time for your client to complete the work, and invite them to share their reflections with you in advance of the session.

❑ Review your client's reflections and consider where you may have additional observations of progress that you can share during the discussion.

❑ Discuss learnings and celebrate!

TOOLS, TEMPLATES, AND EXAMPLES

7-4 CLOSING REFLECTION QUESTIONS

Note: When creating client-facing forms and exercises, include spacing for clients to respond to questions in document.

Coaching Reflections and Plan Forward

Leadership Vision: Insert Your Leadership Vision

First, for each coaching goal:
- What new insights or awareness do you have?
- What progress have you made?
- What are the new habits, behaviors, and mindset that support

---

your success so far?

- What, if anything, is left undone?

- Plan: How will you maintain and evolve your progress?

Then, please answer the following questions about your coaching experience:

1. What are your biggest insights from coaching?

2. What are you most proud of?

3. How would you describe yourself as a leader now? What, if any, refinements do you want to make to your leadership vision?

4. What do you want to focus on as you continue to grow and develop as a leader?

5. How is your life different because of the things you have learned and worked on in coaching?

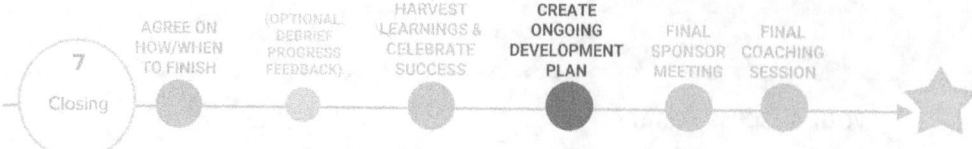

CREATE ONGOING DEVELOPMENT PLAN

CHECKLIST: CREATE ONGOING DEVELOPMENT PLAN

❑ Review your notes and experiences of the client engagement, identifying the key themes, shifts, learnings, and your hunches for the client's ongoing development areas.

❑ Support the client in reviewing their leadership vision, coaching plan, progress feedback (if collected), and learnings about themselves as they consider how they'd like to continue development after coaching ends.

❑ Offer the client a structure to capture their Ongoing Development Plan (7-5).

TOOLS, TEMPLATES, AND EXAMPLES

ONGOING DEVELOPMENT PLAN

An Ongoing Development Plan is similar to the initial coaching goals and plan, with the following content:

For Each Goal:
* Goal
* New insights and awareness
* Successes
* New behaviors/habits/mindsets that support success
* Opportunities for ongoing development
* How to maintain/evolve progress

In addition to the content above, we ask the client to answer the following questions.

1. Beyond the coaching goals, what would the client like to focus on for ongoing development?

2. How can the organization support the client's ongoing development?

7-5 ONGOING DEVELOPMENT PLAN EXAMPLE

Tom's Ongoing Development Plan

Leadership Vision: I will become a more strategic leader who communicates a clear vision and develops my team to lead and execute autonomously.

Goals	Insights	Progress	New Behaviors, Habits & Mindsets	Opportunities for Development	Plan to Maintain
1. From focusing on tactics and "most urgent" to working/ thinking strategically and focusing on "most important"	- Too involved in the execution of things team could do - Different pace/feel to success at this level vs the productivity of "getting things done" - ...	- Mark blocks and protects time for strategic reflection - Delegating 25% of what I used to do to my team - ...	- Team meetings include strategic discussions and priorities review - Weekly review against Eisenhower Matrix - ...	- Further leverage my team as I develop them - Continue to evolve what I do with my strategic thinking time - ...	- Sydney and I to have quarterly check-ins just on my leadership (vs the business) - Ask to be involved in cross-functional strategic initiatives - ...
2. ...	...	...	...	...	...

Ideas for additional development in the next 1–2 years:

- Lead cross-functional strategic initiative to continue to challenge me to think at enterprise level
- Further develop executive presence and find opportunities to present to the Board

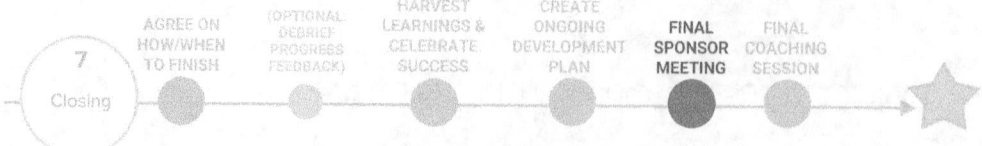

PREPARE CLIENT FOR AND HAVE FINAL SPONSOR MEETING

CHECKLIST: PREPARE CLIENT FOR AND HAVE FINAL SPONSOR MEETING

☐ Prepare your client for the final sponsor meeting (7-6).

☐ Customize the agenda for the final sponsor meeting (7-7).

☐ Email an overview of the meeting (7-8) to the sponsor, outlining the objectives; your client can include any supporting materials they wish to share (e.g., reflection highlights, ongoing development plan, progress feedback).

☐ Support your client and the sponsor in having the wrap-up conversation (per earlier sponsor conversations).

TOOLS, TEMPLATES, AND EXAMPLES

7-6 DISCUSSION GUIDE TO PREPARE A CLIENT FOR THE FINAL SPONSOR MEETING

- How do you want to show up in the meeting with your sponsor? What will you do for the five minutes before the meeting starts to ensure you show up that way?
- What are the key messages (e.g., What are you most proud of from the work?) that you want the sponsor to take away?
- How can your sponsor best support you moving forward? What requests do you have?
- Is there any material (e.g., ongoing development plan) you want to share with the sponsor in advance of meeting?

7- 7 FINAL SPONSOR MEETING AGENDA

As with all sponsor meetings, the client drives the content of the conversation and the coach provides structure, offers supporting comments, and ensures the objectives of the discussion are met.

- Welcome and objectives
- Share themes and insights from Tom's progress feedback assessment
- Discuss Tom's reflections, insights, and ongoing development plan
- Sydney shares her observations and any feedback and/or ideas to strengthen Tom's ongoing development plan
- Discuss any additional ideas to support Tom's ongoing development
- Close with final appreciation for the opportunity

7-8 FINAL SPONSOR MEETING INVITATION EMAIL
Note: This email is written from the client to the client's sponsor.

From: Tom Revere <trevere@usa.lmncorp.com>
To: Sydney Sharpe <ssharpe@usa.lmncorp.com>
Cc: Andie Carlson <andie.carlson@carlsoncoaching.com>
Subject: Coaching- Final Meeting With Andie

Hello Sydney (cc Andie)-

As you know, I am wrapping up my coaching engagement with Andie next month, and as a part of the closing we would like to meet with you to share the results of my progress assessment and my plan for ongoing development after the engagement concludes (both attached).

I will have Mark find a time on your calendar that works well for the three of us.

Many thanks,
Tom

| 7 | AGREE ON HOW/WHEN TO FINISH | (OPTIONAL: DEBRIEF PROGRESS FEEDBACK) | HARVEST LEARNINGS & CELEBRATE SUCCESS | CREATE ONGOING DEVELOPMENT PLAN | FINAL SPONSOR MEETING | FINAL COACHING SESSION |

Closing

COACH CONSIDERATION: We often include a 10,000-mile check-in as part of our engagement; typically 2-3 months after closing. If included, we ask the client to schedule the session when they feel it will best support their ongoing development.

COACH CONSIDERATION: Some coaches send a survey to a client after an engagement concludes to harvest feedback.

FINAL COACHING SESSION

CHECKLIST: FINAL COACHING SESSION

☐ Debrief the sponsor meeting with your client—key takeaways, refinements to the plan, next steps.

☐ Ensure there is time to honor your client's progress and appreciate the time you have had together.

☐ Agree on any follow-on and expectations of one another now that the coaching engagement has wrapped up.

☐ Optional: Ask your client for feedback so you can understand what you've done well and where you could have been even more impactful as the coach.

HONOR THE ENDING WITH COACH CLOSING PRACTICES

CHECKLIST: HONOR THE ENDING WITH COACH CLOSING PRACTICES

☐ Create time to go through your own closing ritual or process for an engagement (7-9)—which may include both reflective activities and process activities (e.g., send a final invoice or close out the client on the tracker).

TOOLS, TEMPLATES, AND EXAMPLES

7-9 COACH CLOSING PRACTICES

Chapter 7 in *DYBC* includes a discussion of the practices to consider as part of your coach closing process. Here is a summary list:

1. Offer a gesture of completion to your client.
2. Wrap up with HR.
3. Summarize the engagement and capture your learnings.
4. Address client notes and another clean-up of the engagement.
5. Celebrate the good work you've done.

> COACH CONSIDERATION: You may consider inviting your client to share a testimonial about working with you as part of your closing practices. Let them know how you'd like to use this—e.g., in your marketing materials.

STICKY SITUATIONS THAT CAN OCCUR WHILE CLOSING A COACHING ENGAGEMENT

STICKY SITUATION	WHAT TO DO
The client doesn't want to collect progress feedback from anyone at the end of the coaching.	Revisit prior discussions and explore resistance. If there are reasonable concerns, consider how to gain this feedback while addressing the client's concerns.
You had a closing meeting with your client but not with the sponsor.	If you have been unsuccessful in organizing a meeting with the sponsor, you can support your client in preparing an email for the sponsor describing the conclusion of the coaching, lessons learned and ongoing development with a request to discuss in their next 1:1. Have the client cc you so you can reply all with any concluding support and comments.

MY NOTES:

The engagement ends without any closing meetings.	If your client goes dark, send an email with concluding support and next steps they can take to feel the engagement has been formally completed.
Too much time has elapsed between the last coaching meeting and the sponsor closing meeting.	If a meeting finally happens, set up the conversation by clearly articulating the timing of when the coaching began and ended to ensure context for evaluating and celebrating the work done in coaching. Be prepared for a more forward-looking conversation as well—and tie things back to learnings from the past months.
A client's direct manager and/or sponsor changes roles shortly before the conclusion of the engagement.	Have a conversation with the client and HR about how to engage the new direct manager and/or sponsor in the closing process. It is essential to engage the client's new direct manager and/or sponsor in the process so that they are aware of the progress the client has made and can support ongoing development.

YOUR TURN

HOW CAN YOU BRING MORE INTENTION TO CLOSING A COACHING ENGAGEMENT?

Reflect on your current practices and the materials shared here.

1. What are you currently doing well?

2. Where would you like to develop, experiment, and/or learn more?

3. I am energized to experiment in these areas:
   a.

   b.

   c.

WHAT TOOLS AND PRACTICES WILL HELP YOU STRENGTHEN THIS ASPECT OF YOUR PRACTICE?

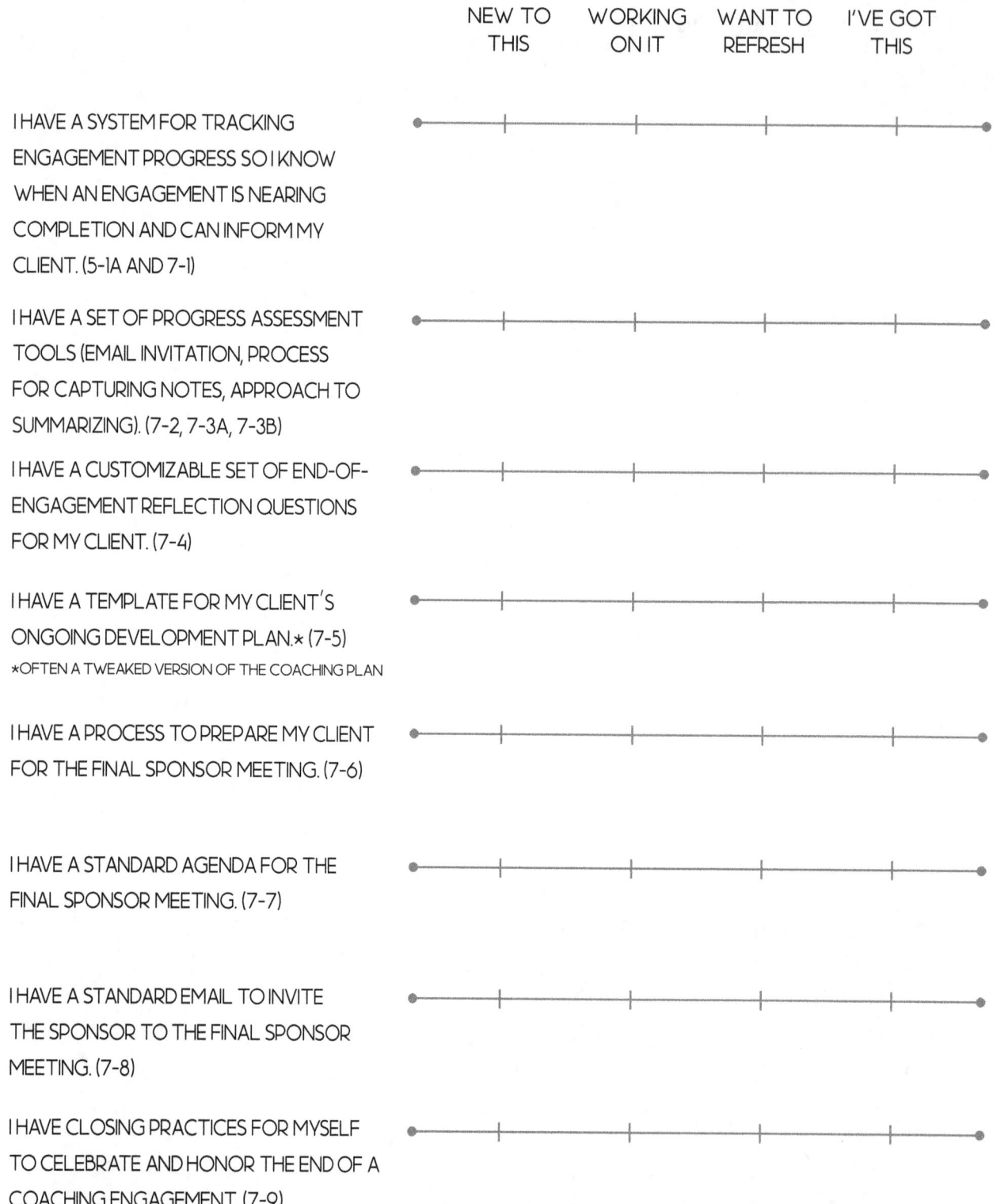

	NEW TO THIS	WORKING ON IT	WANT TO REFRESH	I'VE GOT THIS
I HAVE A SYSTEM FOR TRACKING ENGAGEMENT PROGRESS SO I KNOW WHEN AN ENGAGEMENT IS NEARING COMPLETION AND CAN INFORM MY CLIENT. (5-1A AND 7-1)				
I HAVE A SET OF PROGRESS ASSESSMENT TOOLS (EMAIL INVITATION, PROCESS FOR CAPTURING NOTES, APPROACH TO SUMMARIZING). (7-2, 7-3A, 7-3B)				
I HAVE A CUSTOMIZABLE SET OF END-OF-ENGAGEMENT REFLECTION QUESTIONS FOR MY CLIENT. (7-4)				
I HAVE A TEMPLATE FOR MY CLIENT'S ONGOING DEVELOPMENT PLAN.* (7-5) *OFTEN A TWEAKED VERSION OF THE COACHING PLAN				
I HAVE A PROCESS TO PREPARE MY CLIENT FOR THE FINAL SPONSOR MEETING. (7-6)				
I HAVE A STANDARD AGENDA FOR THE FINAL SPONSOR MEETING. (7-7)				
I HAVE A STANDARD EMAIL TO INVITE THE SPONSOR TO THE FINAL SPONSOR MEETING. (7-8)				
I HAVE CLOSING PRACTICES FOR MYSELF TO CELEBRATE AND HONOR THE END OF A COACHING ENGAGEMENT. (7-9)				

CREATE YOUR PLAN

NOTES		
TIMING		
NEXT STEPS		
TOOL OR APPROACH		

BEYOND THE ENGAGEMENT

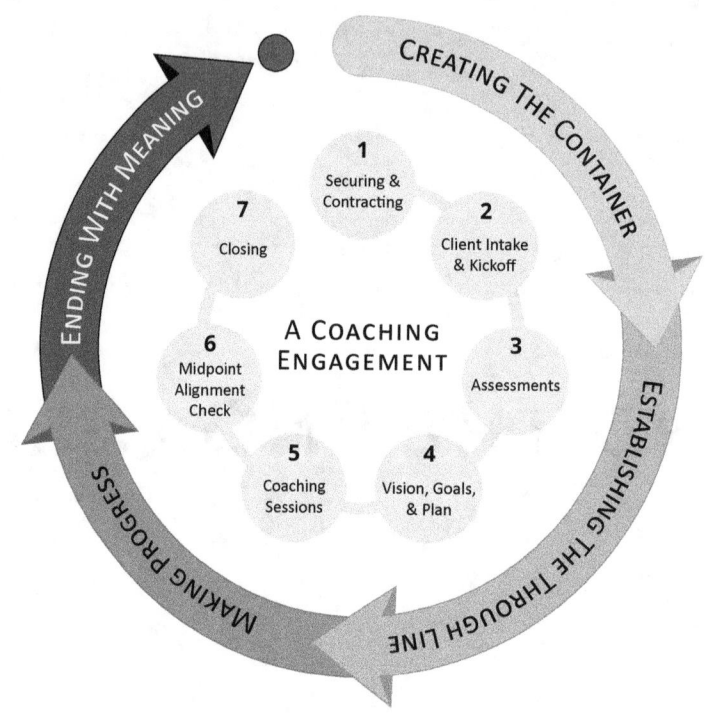

We have now completed the arc
of a coaching engagement.

The next chapters step away from a coaching
engagement and address two topics for bringing
your best you to your coaching work.

CHAPTER 8

YOUR PRESENCE IS AN INTERVENTION: COACHING PRESENCE

Coaching presence is an important component of how clients experience you and ultimately your impact as a coach. In *DYBC* we define coaching presence as the act of attuning to ourselves and our client, of letting go of things outside of the coaching space to be with and witness to the client and our work with them. It's a skill and capacity that can be developed, and we provide many stories and examples of how we and other coaches do this in *DYBC* Chapters 5 and 8.

In this chapter of the workbook, we offer additional ideas for developing the underlying foundation of presence, and how to access your presence before, during, and after coaching conversations. By being intentional about both dimensions—building presence and easily accessing it—you will increase the likelihood of doing your best coaching, and avoiding sticky situations.

KEY OUTCOMES

- An understanding of your presence and ability to access your presence before, during, and after coaching conversations
- A plan for developing and/or sustaining your presence moving forward

DEVELOPING YOUR PRESENCE

CHECKLIST: DEVELOPING YOUR PRESENCE

☐ Assess your presence as it is today (8-1).

☐ If you feel you have a well-developed presence and supporting practices, consider how to sustain and strengthen your presence and practices (see Resources).

☐ If you would like to further develop your presence and supporting practices:

☐ Complete the additional reflection questions below (8-2).

☐ Explore supporting practices that feel consistent with who you are and identify 1–3 practices you wish to experiment with.

☐ Create experiments with new practices, and adjust your approach based on your experiences.

TOOLS, TEMPLATES, AND EXERCISES

8-1 REFLECTION QUESTIONS TO ASSESS YOUR PRESENCE TODAY

What's easy about being fully present with clients?

What's hard about being fully present with clients?

What distracts you from being present to the experience with the client?

How often do you find yourself losing presence during a coaching session?

Do you take time to prepare and presence yourself before coaching sessions?

What practices do you have to deepen or broaden your presence?

What hunches or ideas do you have about how to further expand your capacity to be present? Check in with your gut, then your heart, then your head.

8-2 REFLECTION QUESTIONS TO DEVELOP YOUR PRESENCE

Describe what it would be like to feel fully present in a coaching session. How is that different from how you are today?

Describe what it would look and feel like to your client if you were fully present.

How would increasing your ability to be present impact your coaching work?

What gets in the way of you being as present as you would like to be?

Whose presence do you admire and why?

8-3 IDENTIFY NEW SUPPORTING PRACTICES

How do your colleagues think about and develop presence?

How do your colleagues think about and develop their capacity to be present with clients?

Reach out to individuals who have a presence that you admire and ask what they do to get and stay present. How have they cultivated their presence?

In what ways have you tried to develop your presence in the past? Which of these approaches would you like to bring forward?

Now consider the categories of activities that build presence, and notice which intrigue you. This list is illustrative and not comprehensive:

a. Reflective practices: journaling, meditation, contemplative reading of poetry, intention setting, mindfulness study, labyrinth walking

b. Body practices: yoga, aikido, tai chi, breathwork, embodiment, or somatic training

c. Restorative practices: reiki, acupuncture, massage, retreats

Finally, what are 1–3 practices that you feel attracted to and willing to experiment with?

8-4 CREATE YOUR EXPERIMENTS

Creating experiments is a helpful way to get information about a new approach or practice you believe may be helpful. Below is a well-known and useful approach, the SMART methodology, to set yourself up for successful experiments.

A robust experiment is:
- Specific. In example A below, the experiment is to try one practice (not several).
- Measurable. In both examples, the person experimenting can track if they are/are not sticking with the experiment.
- Achievable. In example B below, the commitment is for 3–4 times a week, not 7 days a week.
- Relevant. Both examples are focused on increasing calm and becoming quieter internally.
- Time bound. Each experiment has a time frame and cadence.

1. Plan your experiments: We share illustrative examples in italics to support your process. Capture your own experiments below these examples.

Idea	Experiment	Hypothesis/Desired Outcome
A. See if a breathing practice will help me be more present before, during, and after coaching sessions.	Do several rounds of box breathing before and after every coaching session. Try it for 2 weeks in July (gives me time to create space between client calls in my calendar for this).	I arrive to sessions more centered and calmer. I'll more easily notice if my client is centered or distracted. I'll be more thoughtful in my post-session reflections.
B. See if I can find a meditation practice that I can sustain, enjoy, and benefit from.	Sign up for a free meditation app and try it out, 3–4 times a week (10 min each time) for 4 weeks this summer. Notice what I like and don't like.	If I stick with meditation enough, I'll begin to experience more calm and better notice my inner state. That awareness will support me being more fully present in coaching.

2. Run your experiment(s)!

3. Reflect on experiments in process and make adjustments to support outcomes (e.g., if 15 minutes of meditation feels too long, shift to 10 minutes)

4. Reflect on outcomes of experiments

 - Notice changes. How are you and your clients benefiting from the work you're doing?

  - Make tweaks. What shifts could further develop your presence? What seems to be missing? What seems to be challenging? What's the next layer of presence you can explore?

PRESENCE BEFORE, DURING, AND AFTER COACHING SESSIONS

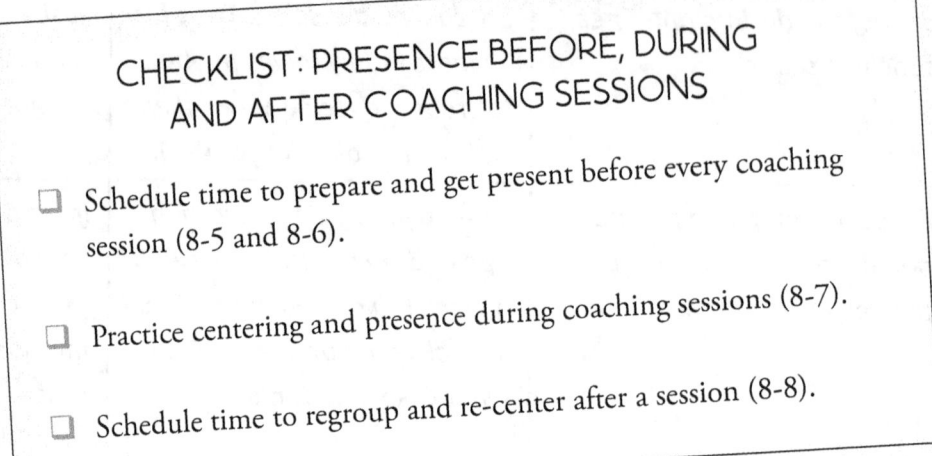

CHECKLIST: PRESENCE BEFORE, DURING AND AFTER COACHING SESSIONS

☐ Schedule time to prepare and get present before every coaching session (8-5 and 8-6).

☐ Practice centering and presence during coaching sessions (8-7).

☐ Schedule time to regroup and re-center after a session (8-8).

TOOLS, TEMPLATES, AND EXERCISES

SHORTER PRESENCING PRACTICES BEFORE A COACHING SESSION

Adopt a 2-to-5-minute practice to help you get centered and ready to focus on your client and the coaching. We offer several examples below. Please proceed cautiously with the breathing practices, as some may require building up over time.

8-5a CENTERED BREATHING

This example is inspired by Wendy and Tiphani Palmer of Leadership Embodiment. It can take as little as 20 seconds or as long as a couple of minutes.
   a. Inhale, lengthening your spine.
   b. Exhale, relaxing your muscles and thinking of something that makes you smile, without losing the length in your spine.
   c. Look to the floor, ceiling, and four corners of your room, then energetically expand and settle into the space.

8-5b BOX BREATHING

This example is also referred to as Square Breathing, famously used by US Navy Seals.

    a. Inhale through your nose while counting to four.

    b. Hold your breath while counting to four.

    c. Exhale while counting to four.

    d. Hold your breath while counting to four.

    e. Repeat multiple times.

8-5c 4-7-8 BREATHING

    a. Place your tongue on the roof of your mouth and leave it there during this exercise.

    b. Release your calf muscles—you can do this by bending your knees or sitting. Maintain this position.

    c. Inhale through your nose while counting to four.

    d. Hold your breath while counting to seven.

    e. Exhale through pursed lips, making a whoosh sound, while counting to eight.

    f. Repeat three times for a total of four cycles.

8-5d INTENTION SETTING

    a. Pause and bring your client to mind.

    b. Consider how you want to be with this client. Bring some words or mental image or metaphor to mind that reflects how you want to be.

    c. Carry this with you into the conversation.

LONGER PRESENCING PRACTICES BEFORE A COACHING SESSION

It's helpful to have a longer presencing practice in your repertoire for times when you know you need more than a short practice to effectively shift your presence.

8-6a BREATHING PRACTICES

Cultivate a longer version of your regular practice (e.g., centered breathing) that you can easily access, depending on the time you have before a coaching conversation.

8-6b GUIDED MEDITATION

You may already have a meditation practice you can adapt for use before client meetings. If not, using an app is an easy way to access guided meditation. Apps we've used include Headspace, Calm, and Insight Timer. An app that allows you to save favorites and filter by time is helpful for the purposes of pre-client meeting preparation.

8-7 PRESENCE DURING COACHING SESSIONS

We all have moments when we lose presence with a client. Typically, we can quickly regain presence by "catching ourselves in the act" and deliberately becoming present to the client in the moment. Be intentional about how you want to navigate those moments by reflecting on these questions:

- What helps you notice when you have disconnected? What allows you to come back to being present?

- How might you use those moments when your presence isn't what you want it to be, whether the client feels the disconnect or not? For example:
  - Consider if there is learning in your disconnect from your client. If so, how can you use immediacy to share this observation with your client in a way that they can hear and understand it?
  - Track moments of disconnection to help you notice potential patterns and blind spots.

8-8 REGROUP AND RE-CENTER AFTER A COACHING SESSION

Consider how you re-center after a coaching conversation, while not losing the lingering hunches, insights, and observations that will feed your reflection of the conversation and the client.

What's the practice that will help you notice and release any residual energy? For example:
- Taking a few notes
- Taking a few breaths
- Moving from one room to another or going outside
- Moving your body in a different way (e.g., standing up, stretching, or walking)
- Other_____

Play around with what works for you and the order that best serves your work (e.g., capturing session notes first or re-centering first?).

STICKY SITUATIONS THAT CAN BE PREVENTED
WITH GREATER COACHING PRESENCE

STICKY SITUATION	WHAT TO DO
You find yourself entering coaching sessions without preparation and intentional presence.	See Chapter 5 Sticky Situations, What to Do
You have trouble maintaining your presence in coaching sessions.	See Chapter 5 Sticky Situations, What to Do Experiment with activities that help you build your foundational presence (e.g., journaling, meditation, being in nature, yoga …).
Your ability to access and maintain your presence is suffering because you are overextended.	See Chapter 1 Sticky Situations, What to Do See Chapter 5 Sticky Situations, What to Do Experiment with activities that help you build your foundational presence (e.g., journaling, meditation, being in nature, yoga …).

RESOURCES FOR DEVELOPING PRESENCE

These are a few of our favorite resources and teachers. Many of these authors and teachers have multiple books, articles and programs to explore:

- *Buddha's Brain: The Practical Neuroscience of Happiness, Love and Wisdom,* by Rick Hanson with Richard Mendius
- *A Gestalt Coaching Primer: The Path towards Awareness Intelligence,* by Dorothy Siminovitch
- *Leadership Embodiment: How the Way We Sit and Stand Can Change the Way We Think and Speak,* by Wendy Palmer and Janet Crawford

- *Presence: Human Purpose and the Field of the Future,* by Peter Senge, Otto Scharmer, and Joseph Jaworski
- *Presence-Based Coaching and The Mindful Coach,* by Doug Silsbee
- *Self as Coach, Self as Leader,* by Pamela McLean (Chapter 4 in particular)
- *The Book of Awakening,* by Mark Nepo
- *Your Body Is Your Brain,* by Amanda Blake
- David Whyte: davidwhyte.com/
- Tara Brach: tarabrach.com/
- Tiphani Palmer: leadershipembodiment.com/
- The Strozzi Institute: strozziinstitute.com/

What resources would you add to this list?

YOUR TURN

HOW CAN YOU DEVELOP YOUR COACHING PRESENCE?
Reflect on your current practices and the materials shared here.

1. What are you currently doing well?

2. Where would you like to develop, experiment, and/or learn more?

3. I am energized to experiment in these areas:
   a.

   b.

   c.

WHAT TOOLS AND PRACTICES WILL HELP YOU STRENGTHEN THIS ASPECT OF YOUR PRACTICE?

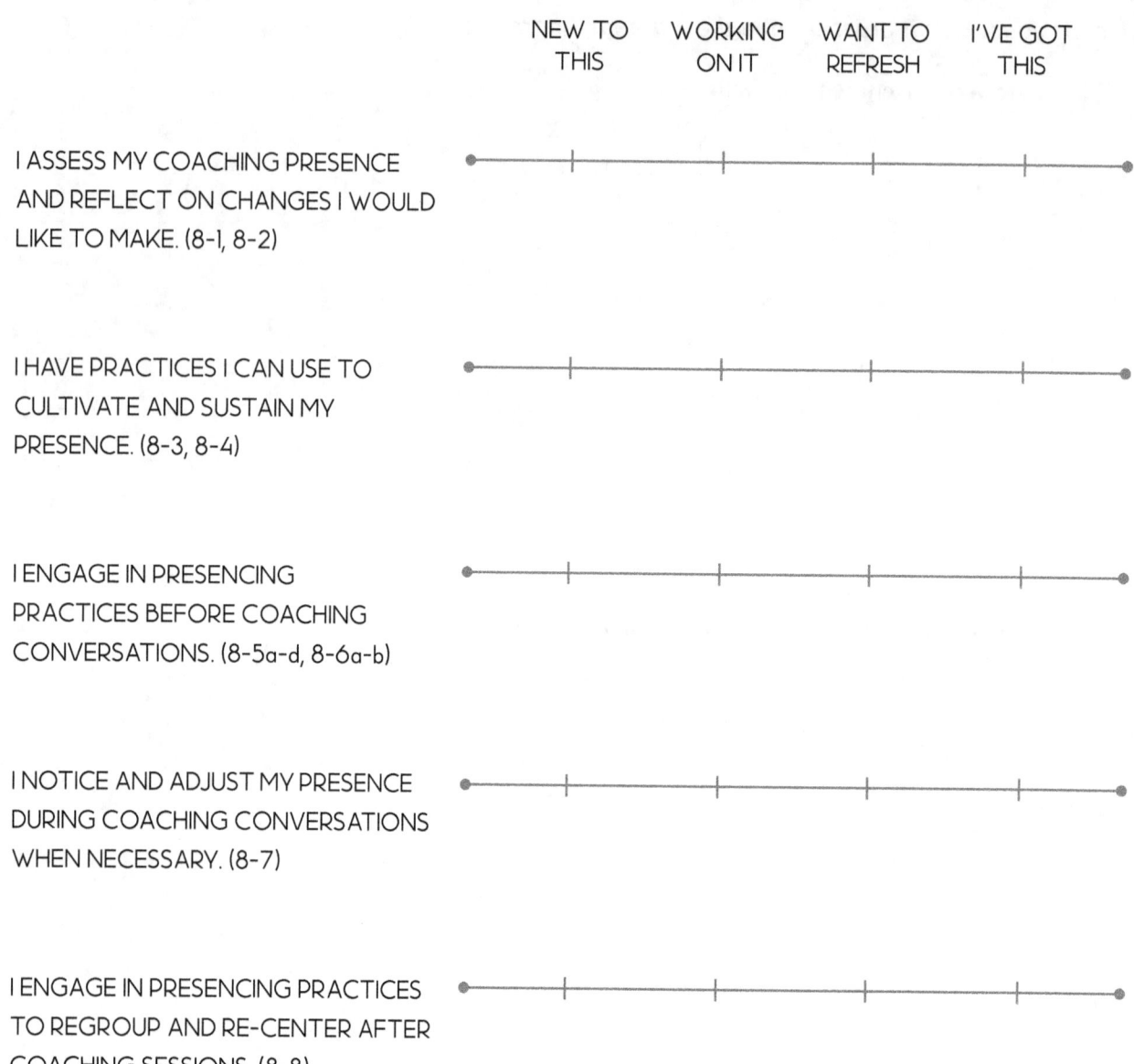

	NEW TO THIS	WORKING ON IT	WANT TO REFRESH	I'VE GOT THIS
I ASSESS MY COACHING PRESENCE AND REFLECT ON CHANGES I WOULD LIKE TO MAKE. (8-1, 8-2)				
I HAVE PRACTICES I CAN USE TO CULTIVATE AND SUSTAIN MY PRESENCE. (8-3, 8-4)				
I ENGAGE IN PRESENCING PRACTICES BEFORE COACHING CONVERSATIONS. (8-5a-d, 8-6a-b)				
I NOTICE AND ADJUST MY PRESENCE DURING COACHING CONVERSATIONS WHEN NECESSARY. (8-7)				
I ENGAGE IN PRESENCING PRACTICES TO REGROUP AND RE-CENTER AFTER COACHING SESSIONS. (8-8)				

CREATE YOUR PLAN

NOTES			
TIMING			
NEXT STEPS			
TOOL OR APPROACH			

CHAPTER 9

YOU ARE YOUR OWN BEST TOOL: ONGOING DEVELOPMENT FOR COACHES

If you are the most important tool in your coaching toolbox, how can you continue to bring your best self to your clients and your coaching? Most coaches we know engage in planning activities annually (at a minimum). Often, this begins with reflecting and assessing the business end of their practice (e.g., number and types of clients, sources of clients, revenue, etc.). This is then followed by reflecting on the experience of the past year and considering how to move ahead with intention. From this foundation, you can create your strategy for your ongoing development as a coach.

If this feels similar to the work you do with clients, that's because it is. Coaches offer clients the space to reflect on who they are today and create a vision for the future. They then support clients in bringing that vision to life. And, as clients turn to coaches for support and guidance, you may also find additional support helpful (e.g., working with a peer as an accountability partner or formally engaging a coach or a coach supervisor).

KEY OUTCOMES

- Meaningful reflection on who you are as a coach today
- A vision for the future to fuel your development plan
- A strategy and plan for ongoing development that supports your desired vision

Here is a simple process for considering and planning for your own development as a coach:

Step 1: Reflect, Review and Integrate

Step 2: Ideate and Research

Step 3: Strategize and Plan

STEP 1: REFLECT, REVIEW, AND INTEGRATE

Many coaches revisit and refresh this work periodically throughout the year. Select the cadence that feels right to you.

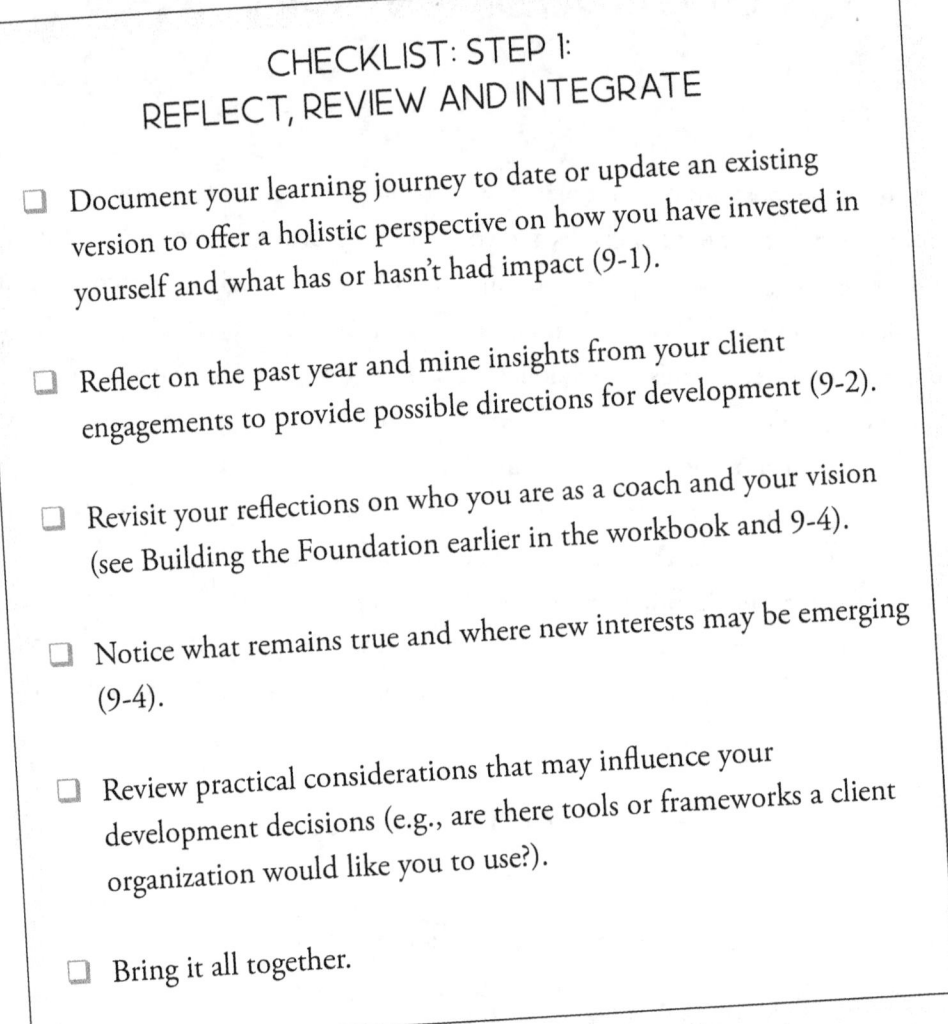

CHECKLIST: STEP 1:
REFLECT, REVIEW AND INTEGRATE

☐ Document your learning journey to date or update an existing version to offer a holistic perspective on how you have invested in yourself and what has or hasn't had impact (9-1).

☐ Reflect on the past year and mine insights from your client engagements to provide possible directions for development (9-2).

☐ Revisit your reflections on who you are as a coach and your vision (see Building the Foundation earlier in the workbook and 9-4).

☐ Notice what remains true and where new interests may be emerging (9-4).

☐ Review practical considerations that may influence your development decisions (e.g., are there tools or frameworks a client organization would like you to use?).

☐ Bring it all together.

TOOLS, TEMPLATES, AND PRACTICES

Below are multiple ways to mine your past experience and reflections to inform your development plan. You may choose to do all of these or select those that are most compelling for you at this time.

CAPTURE YOUR LEARNING JOURNEY AND KEY INSIGHTS

Taking the time to reflect upon and document your learning journey is a useful starting point to create an ongoing development strategy and plan. It can also be a fun walk down memory lane as many of the learning activities we engage in are in community with other coaches who become colleagues and often friends.

Documenting your journey-to-date surfaces themes or trends (e.g., areas of interest, opportunities to augment or rebalance your development). As you capture the types of learning and the modalities you have engaged in, it's easier to identify what has been most impactful and satisfying to you.

There are many ways to reflect. Two possibilities are:

9-1a LEARNING JOURNEY—LIFELINE APPROACH (OPTION 1)

Create a Learning Journey Lifeline

Adapt a traditional lifeline exercise to focus purely on your development:
1. Reflect on the development activities you have experienced as a coach. This can include formal learning (e.g., classes) and informal learning (e.g., book clubs).
2. Capture the events on the next page using the template provided. Starting at the beginning of your coaching journey, place the experiences in order chronologically.
   a. Annotate each experience with a brief description and the year it occurred.
   b. Consider using different colors or sizes of symbols to differentiate the experiences (e.g., size of the investment or different types of learning).
   c. Use distance from the midline to represent the degree of impact on your development.
      i. Experiences that were positive/impactful/satisfying go above the line. The farther the distance from the line, the better the event.
      ii. Experiences that were negative/unimpactful/unsatisfying go below the line. The farther the distance from the line, the more challenging the event.
3. Finally, connect the experiences with lines to show your experience over the years.

> COACH CONSIDERATION: You may choose a different starting point if you've been coaching for many years, or if your work prior to coaching was rich with development activities that inform your coaching.

LEARNING JOURNEY TEMPLATE

Time

Level of
Impact/
Satisfaction

+

Neutral

|

9-1b LEARNING JOURNEY—INVENTORY APPROACH (OPTION 2)

Create an inventory from your learning journey.

This method provides the opportunity to notice the different modalities (e.g., virtual or in person; individual or in groups; reading, discussing, being taught, practicing), as well as the degree of time and attention you have invested year by year.

The example below captures the type of development, the topics, and the "overall learning gear," which can be helpful because our ability to invest our time, attention, and financial resources ebbs and flows based on multiple factors.

When starting this activity, take the time to consider the categories that will be most useful to you.

ANDIE'S LEARNING JOURNEY INVENTORY

LEARNING JOURNEY						
Year	Super-vision	Learning Confer-ences	Assess-ments	Personal Growth	Coaching Topics & Tools	Overall Learning Gear
2018	Group	Hudson	Team Diagnostic Assessment		Presence-Based Coaching	Exploring
2019	Group	Hudson, IOC	The Learning Circle Profile	Embodiment training and coach certification		Intense Learning
2020	Group	Hudson		Study with: David Whyte	Neuro-science of Embodi-ment	Integrat-ing
2021	Group	IOC		Mark Nepo	Somatics refresh	Exploring
2022	Group	Hudson	iEQ9 Enneagram		Polarities	Intense Learning

> COACH CONSIDERATION: A coach's ability and desire to engage in development changes from year to year. Some years are intense in terms of actively engaging in learning or going deep in a topic; others are times of integration of learning; and finally, others may be filled with learning in a lighter way. It can be helpful to step back and notice patterns as an input to your planning process.

9-1c REFLECT ON YOUR LEARNING JOURNEY

Once you have documented your learning journey, step back and consider where you are in your development journey as a coach. Newer coaches might consider focusing on creating a foundation—the baseline assessment, frameworks, and approaches that will support their coaching. A coach who has a foundation in place may seek development in more specialized areas.

What themes do you notice across your learning journey?

What have been the most impactful development activities? Why?

Which activities have had the most powerful impact on how you coach? Why?

Which activities were not useful? Why?

What learning formats are most satisfying to you (e.g., learning with others, self-directed, in-person, virtual ...)?

To what degree have you integrated and implemented your learning?

9-2 COACH YEAR IN REVIEW REFLECTION

Review and reflect on the last 12 months. You may consider referencing resources such as Pamela McLean's Self as Coach model (9-3) and the ICF and/or EMCC Competencies models to ensure that you consider multiple aspects of your work as a coach (see Appendix):

What are you most proud of this year? Why?

What (if anything) makes you wish you could have a "do-over"? Why?

Are there any "sticky situations" that you noticed coming up repeatedly?

Where do you think you are strongest as a coach today?

Where do you see opportunities to develop?

What insights have you gained from the feedback you've received?

What aspects of coaching are you curious to learn more about? Why?

What aspects of coaching are you prepared to leave behind? Why?

9-3 SELF AS COACH MODEL

We frequently refer to a self-development model for coaches put forth in the book *Self as Coach, Self as Leader* by Pamela McLean. The Self as Coach model focuses on six dimensions that are essential to coaches, and is a useful way to identify current learning edges:

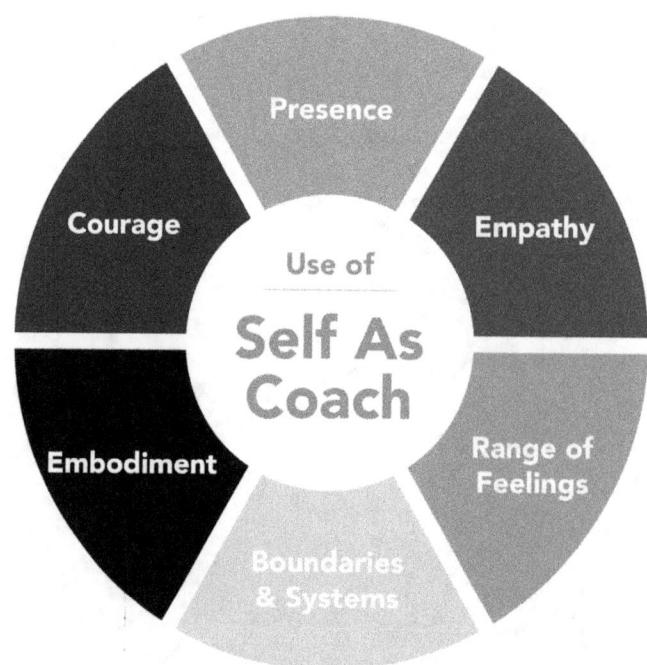

9-4 REVISIT AND REFRESH WHO YOU ARE AS A COACH AND YOUR VISION FOR THE FUTURE

Pull out your reflections and responses to the Building the Foundation exercises at the beginning of this workbook and review them. Then consider the following questions:

What's changed since you last did that reflection work? What remains the same?

What do you want to expand, edit, or eliminate?

Is your vision still accurate and compelling to you? If not, what adjustments would make your vision compelling again?

What gaps between what's true now and your vision for the future do you want to address?

STEP 2: IDEATE AND RESEARCH

Now, it's time to identify and research programs that will help you bring your plan into reality. We are frequently engaged in conversations with our peers about the learning they are doing, and we keep a running wish list of development options, opportunities to learn along with others and from proven teachers, and ways to broaden our toolkit as coaches as well as for our own personal growth.

CHECKLIST: ONGOING DEVELOPMENT: IDEATE AND RESEARCH

☐ Identify the development categories and programs that will support you in moving toward your vision of who you want to be as a coach and your ideal practice (9-5).

☐ Research possible programs and experiences that support your vision and your practice (9-6 and 9-7).

TOOLS, TEMPLATES, AND EXAMPLES

9-5 LEARNING DEVELOPMENT IDEATION EXERCISE

Now that you have a clear view of your learning journey, the insights you have harvested, and a clear vision for the year ahead, bring them together and consider what type of development will support your journey to achieving your vision:

Where do I want to take my coaching practice in the next few years, and what learning will support me in achieving this vision?

What feedback am I getting from clients about my coaching and how can that inform my development plan?

What development will make me a better coach for my clients moving forward?

What tools or frameworks have I heard about from colleagues or research that have piqued my curiosity?

Are there tools or frameworks that client organizations (or my organization) would like me to use?

What time, energy, and money can I devote to my development this year?

How do I need to pace my learning activities, given my personal and professional commitments in the year(s) ahead?

What are the opportunities to learn with my colleagues and build community?

What topics are most interesting to me right now?

9-6 RESEARCH POTENTIAL DEVELOPMENT OPPORTUNITIES

As you integrate all of the insights you have harvested, a clear path forward may come easily to you, but if it does not, consider the following resources:

- Review the table of categories and examples of coach development (9-7).
- Take note of podcasts, articles, and books you have read that discuss available development opportunities.
- Identify trusted individuals you can talk with to gain perspective on development possibilities. This may include:
  - Coaches you respect who are on a similar path
  - Mentors or supervisors
  - Former teachers

9-7 CATEGORIES AND EXAMPLES OF COACH DEVELOPMENT (ILLUSTRATIVE, NOT EXHAUSTIVE)

COACHING TOOLS & FRAMEWORKS				
SELF-DEVELOPMENT	EXPANDING & STRENGTHENING COACHING CAPABILITIES	LEADERSHIP ASSESSMENTS	DIAGNOSTIC TOOLS	FRAMEWORKS & TOOLS TO SUPPORT A COACHING CONVERSATION
• Creativity classes	• Brain-based coaching programs	• Be Well, Lead Well	• Clifton Strengths	• Daring Greatly
• Embodiment/Somatics	• Depth coaching programs	• Hogan Assessments	• DiSC	• Immunity to Change
• Reflection workshops with thought leaders (e.g., Mark Nepo)	• Master coach programs	• The Leadership Circle Profile	• Enneagram	• Metaphor Magic
• Self as coach work	• Positive psychology degree programs	• The Leadership Effectiveness Analysis	• EQ in Action	• Neuro-Linguistic Programming
…	…	…	• Insights Discovery	• Theory U
			• Myers-Briggs Type Indicator	…
			…	

DEVELOPMENT ACTIVITIES THAT OFFER ENRICHMENT ACROSS CATEGORIES:

Coaching Conferences (e.g., ICF Converge,
EMCC Global Coaching & Supervision Conference, etc.)

Coaching Supervision (1:1 or group)

STEP 3: STRATEGIZE AND PLAN

CHECKLIST: ONGOING DEVELOPMENT: STRATEGIZE AND PLAN

☐ Create your development plan for the year ahead. Consider what times of year are best for you to carve out for your development, especially if you want to undertake an intensive learning experience (9-8).

TOOLS, TEMPLATES, AND EXAMPLES

9-8 LEARNING PLAN FOR AN EXPERIENCED COACH

> **COACH CONSIDERATION:** Pull your vision forward from the work you have done and use it to inspire you as you create and use your learning plan.

My Coaching Vision: I work with vibrant leaders and changemakers who are passionate about growing their impact and leading their organizations to new heights of excellence. My clients love learning, are willing to experiment in order to grow, and work with me for 6- to 12-month engagements

Learning Intention: I stay on the top of my game by continuing to learn about new tools that will support my clients, reading voraciously, and intentionally pursuing my personal path of adult development.

Q1	Q2	Q3	Q4
Group Supervision			
Intro to Tai Chi (Wed evenings in Feb)	Leadership Circle Profile certification (May 2023)	Integration time (no formal class participation)	Neuro-Linguistic Programming (date and course tbd)

Other resources to support my learning:

Books I want to read:
- *Feedback Reimagined,* by Peter Berridge and Jen Ostrich
- *Six Paths to Leadership,* by Meredith Persily and Mark A. Clark
- *The Leader You Want to Be,* by Amy Jen Su
- *Your Invisible Network,* by Michael Melcher

Podcasts I want to listen to:
Coaching Real Leaders with Muriel Wilkins

Conferences I want to attend:
Institute of Coaching

Thought leadership I want to follow:
Pam McLean
David Clutterbuck
Adam Grant
McKinsey Quarterly
HBR

We encourage you to have a plan, but not to be overly anchored to it as new opportunities and needs may emerge over the year.

YOUR TURN

HOW CAN YOU BRING MORE INTENTION TO YOUR OWN DEVELOPMENT AS A COACH?

Reflect on your current practices and the materials shared here.

1. What are you currently doing well?

2. Where would you like to develop, experiment, and/or learn more?

3. I am energized to experiment in these areas:

    a.

    b.

    c.

WHAT TOOLS AND PRACTICES WILL HELP YOU STRENGTHEN THIS ASPECT OF YOUR PRACTICE?

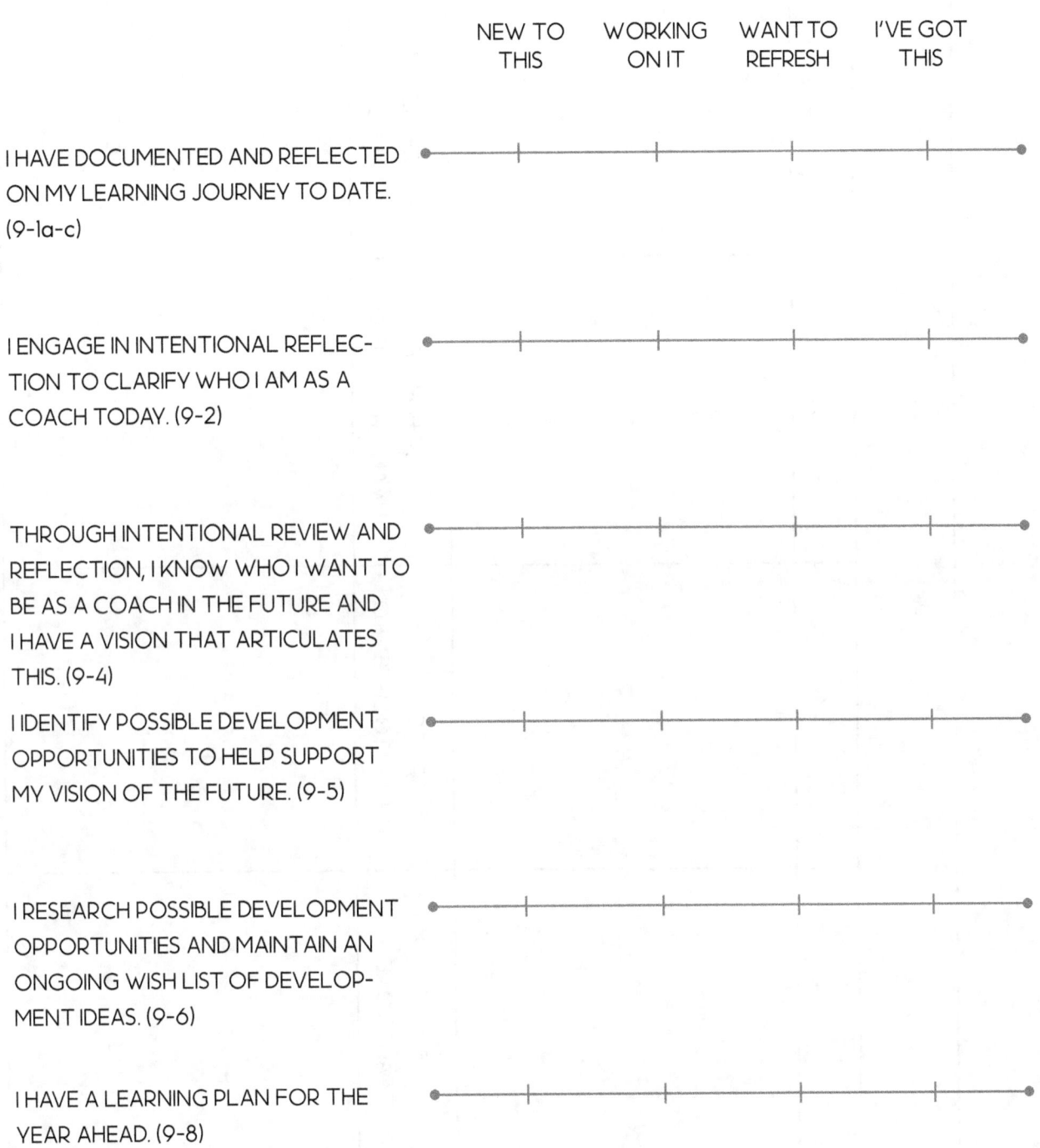

	NEW TO THIS	WORKING ON IT	WANT TO REFRESH	I'VE GOT THIS
I HAVE DOCUMENTED AND REFLECTED ON MY LEARNING JOURNEY TO DATE. (9-1a-c)				
I ENGAGE IN INTENTIONAL REFLECTION TO CLARIFY WHO I AM AS A COACH TODAY. (9-2)				
THROUGH INTENTIONAL REVIEW AND REFLECTION, I KNOW WHO I WANT TO BE AS A COACH IN THE FUTURE AND I HAVE A VISION THAT ARTICULATES THIS. (9-4)				
I IDENTIFY POSSIBLE DEVELOPMENT OPPORTUNITIES TO HELP SUPPORT MY VISION OF THE FUTURE. (9-5)				
I RESEARCH POSSIBLE DEVELOPMENT OPPORTUNITIES AND MAINTAIN AN ONGOING WISH LIST OF DEVELOPMENT IDEAS. (9-6)				
I HAVE A LEARNING PLAN FOR THE YEAR AHEAD. (9-8)				

CREATE YOUR LEARNING PLAN

MY COACHING VISION	MY LEARNING INTENTION	LEARNING BY QUARTER				
			Q1	Q2	Q3	Q4
		RESOURCES TO SUPPORT MY LEARNING	BOOKS I WANT TO READ	PODCASTS I WANT TO LISTEN TO	CONFERENCES I WANT TO ATTEND	THOUGHT LEADERSHIP I WANT TO FOLLOW

AFTERWORD

Thank you for reading *Do Your Best Coaching: The Workbook!*

When we published *Do Your Best Coaching: Navigating a Coaching Engagement From Start To Finish* in 2022, one of the most frequent questions we fielded was "What is it like to write a book with a co-author?" Our immediate response then (and now!) is that we could not imagine doing it any other way. Fast-forward a year, and now as we prepare to publish this workbook in 2023, the most frequent question we're fielding is "What is it like to write two books in two years?" Our answer to that is "A LOT!" But here too we could not imagine doing it any other way.

When we began this journey, our hope was to write a book (now two) that would support new coaches to launch their practices with more confidence and less uncertainty, and to inspire experienced coaches to reflect on their practice and experiment with what captures their imagination. However, we had no idea the impact it would have on each of us.

Over the past two years we've had the pleasure of interviewing and learning from coaches across the globe. We've also had the opportunity to convene groups of coaches to explore intentional engagement and build learning communities. We often comment on how much our own coaching has improved through researching and writing these books as well as the many discussions we have had with coaches since then. Our community has expanded in a way we could not have imagined, and for that we are grateful.

We hope you've enjoyed *DYBC: The Workbook* and that it helps you approach coaching engagements with intention, increase your coaching impact, and avoid sticky situations.

If you would like to receive updates from us, including free downloadable resources, please join our mailing list or visit our website: www.DoYourBestCoaching.com

Finally, one of our passions is supporting coaches to develop and to engage in meaningful conversations with each other. If you have found value in *DYBC* please consider leaving a review on Amazon, which will help other readers find the book more easily.

Thank you!

Julie and Laura

www.doyourbestcoaching.com

linkedin.com/in/juliehess

linkedin.com/in/lauradaleycoach

APPENDIX

COACH SELF-ASSESSMENT: HOW ARE YOU INTENTIONALLY ENGAGING?

We invite you to reflect on your current approach to coaching engagements and notice where you are doing well and where you may want to augment or refresh your approach.

Each section of the coach self-assessment relates to a phase of the Intentional Engagement Framework Phase, and its corresponding process steps, allowing you to dive into this workbook or *DYBC* for further exploration. You can also download this assessment as a fillable pdf on our website: www.doyourbestcoaching.com

HOW ARE YOU INTENTIONALLY ENGAGING?

PHASE I

Defining ways of working with your client and the organization and developing the safe space and trust required in an impactful coaching relationship.

	NEW TO THIS	WORKING ON IT	WANT TO REFRESH	I'VE GOT THIS
I prepare thoroughly for chemistry calls.				
I establish confidentiality and boundaries with the client and the organization.				
I create alignment on the coaching process, roles and responsibilities with the client and the organization.				
I use a purposeful intake process to deepen the client's self-awareness and to build our relationship.				
I balance foundational relationship building with time-sensitive coaching needs.				

CREATING THE CONTAINER

1 Securing & Contracting
2 Client Intake & Kickoff

PHASE II

Clarifying where the client is today, what future success looks like personally and professionally, and the meaningful goals and coaching plan that will help them get from here to there.

	NEW TO THIS	WORKING ON IT	WANT TO REFRESH	I'VE GOT THIS
I craft an assessment strategy to expand the client's awareness while aligning with organizational preferences.				
I prepare myself to debrief assessment results in a way that best serves the client.				
I thoughtfully prepare my client to receive assessment results prior to the debrief.				
I support the client to develop a vision of their future and integrate it with assessment insights to create meaningful goals and a coaching plan.				
I work with the client to engage their sponsor in a discussion to align on their goals and coaching plan.				

ESTABLISHING THE THROUGH LINE

3 Assessments
4 Vision, Goals, & Plan

PHASE III

Coaching clients to make the changes they aspire to, while checking for alignment with the client and the organization. Great coaching coupled with alignment touch points leads to clarity regarding success and client progress.

	NEW TO THIS	WORKING ON IT	WANT TO REFRESH	I'VE GOT THIS
I manage my practice capacity and schedule to ensure I can be fully present with each client.				
I prepare prior to and reflect after each coaching session.				
I observe my client's presence at the start of every session and support them to shift into a coaching mindset when appropriate.				
I maintain presence throughout each coaching session so I can attend to the work.				
I regularly check-in throughout the engagement to ensure the client and I are aligned on our work.				
The client and I check-in with their sponsor to ensure ongoing alignment.				

MAKING PROGRESS

5 Coaching Sessions
6 Midpoint Alignment Check

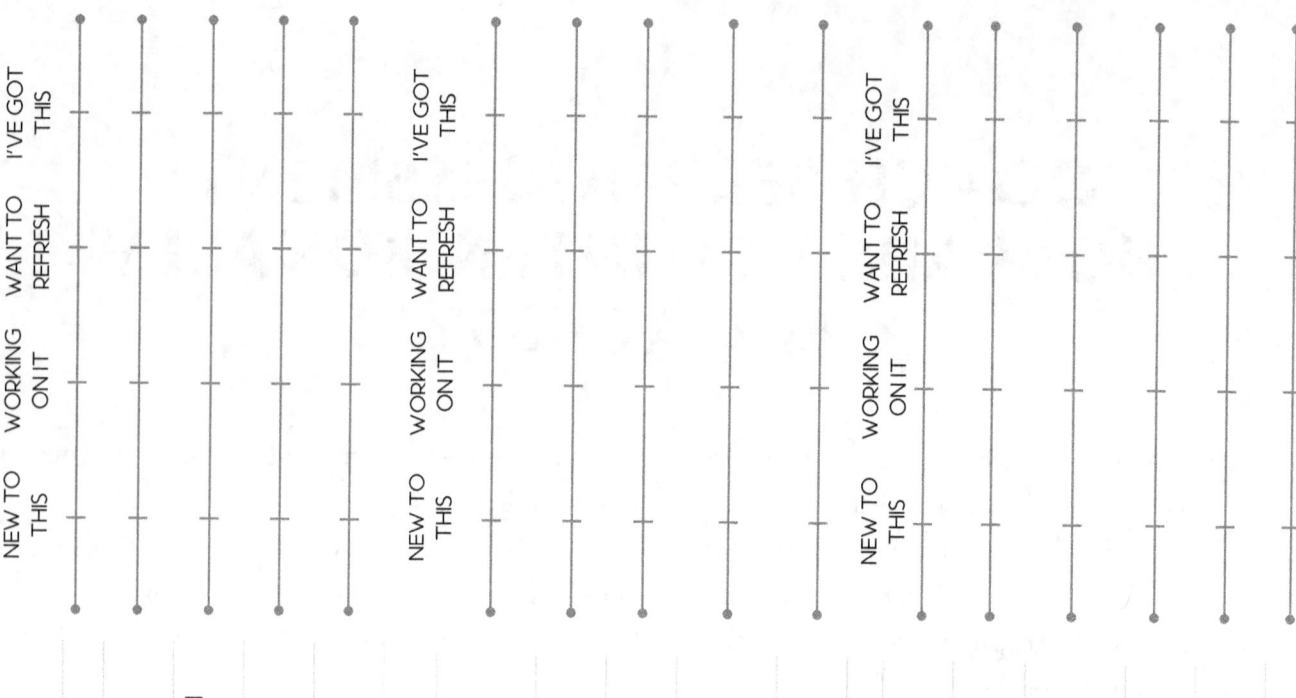

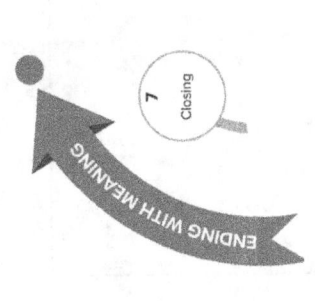

ENDING WITH MEANING

7 Closing

PHASE IV

Supporting the client and the organization to reflect on the work that has been done, celebrate the client's progress, and plan for the future. A strong finish creates a smooth transition out of coaching into continued growth.

	NEW TO THIS	WORKING ON IT	WANT TO REFRESH	I'VE GOT THIS
I track engagements and proactively prepare the client and the organization for the end of the engagement.				
I engage the client in meaningful reflection to harvest learnings and celebrate progress.				
I work with the client to create an ongoing development plan that builds on the progress made.				
I support the client and sponsor to prepare and come together for a closing meeting to recognize progress made and confirm organizational support moving forward.				

BEYOND THE ENGAGEMENT: COACHING PRESENCE

	NEW TO THIS	WORKING ON IT	WANT TO REFRESH	I'VE GOT THIS
I have regular practices to support my ongoing presence				
I pause and employ practices to be present before, during and after a coaching session				
I take opportunities to learn about and grow my ability to be present				

BEYOND THE ENGAGEMENT: ONGOING DEVELOPMENT

	NEW TO THIS	WORKING ON IT	WANT TO REFRESH	I'VE GOT THIS
I regularly reflect and take stock of my strengths and challenges to fuel future development				
I have created an ongoing development strategy that I review and refresh periodically				
I actively engage in learning communities to support my own development				

NOW PAUSE & CONSIDER

Where am I engaging intentionally today?

Where do I see opportunities to increase intentionality?

I am energized around experimenting in these areas:

1.

2.

3.

DO YOUR BEST COACHING: THE ILLUSTRATED PROCESS FROM START TO FINISH

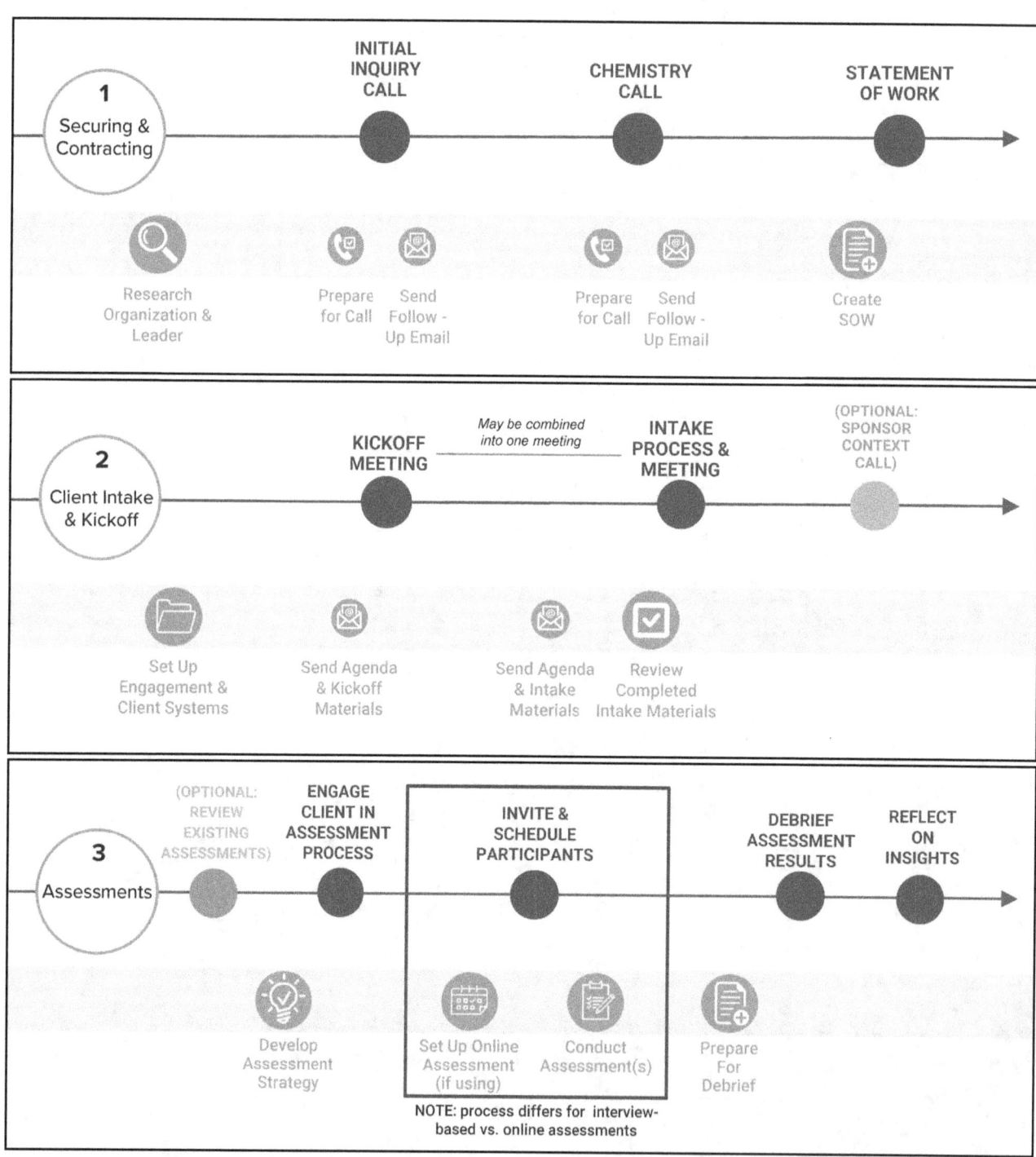

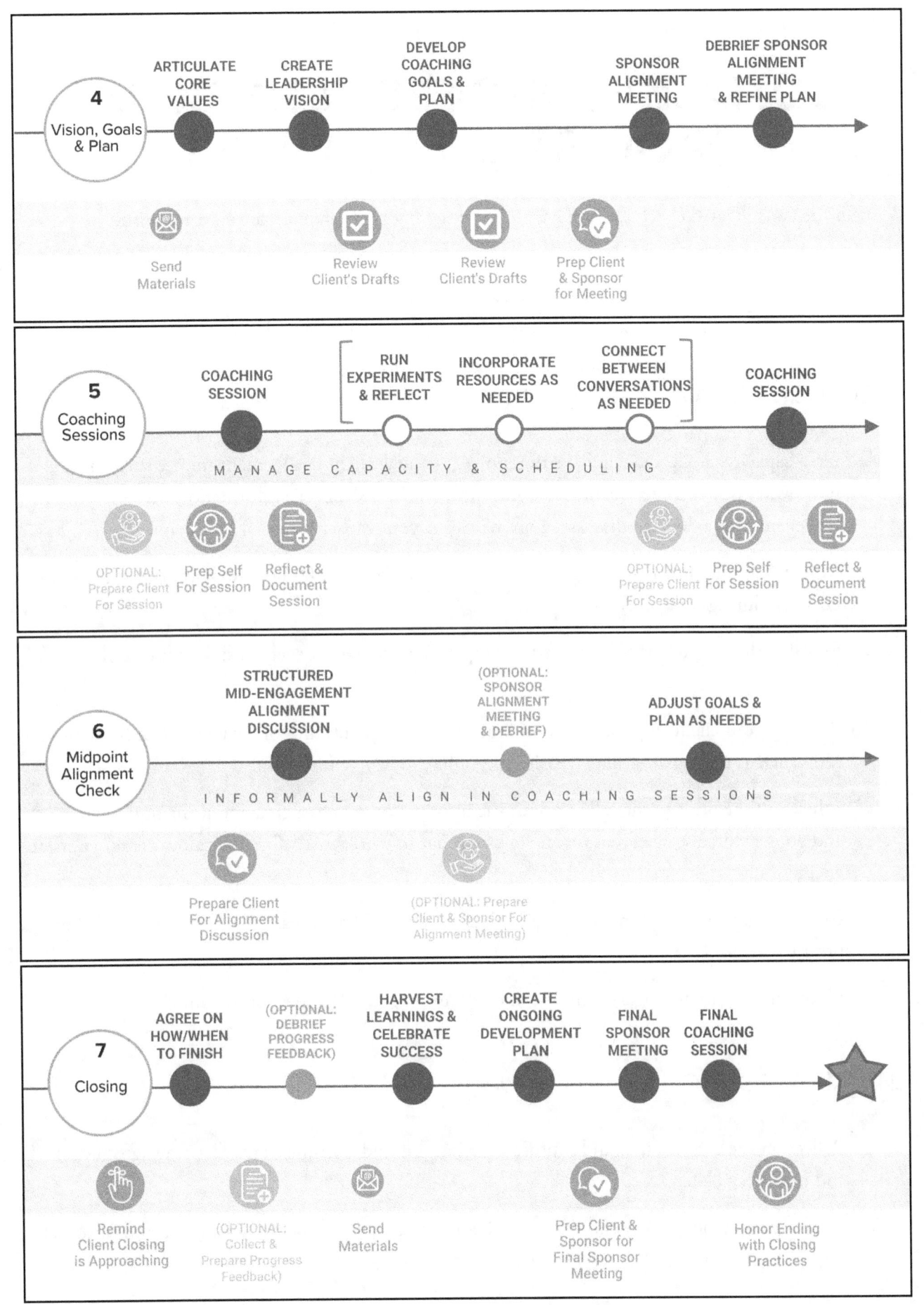

4 — Vision, Goals & Plan

ARTICULATE CORE VALUES • CREATE LEADERSHIP VISION • DEVELOP COACHING GOALS & PLAN • SPONSOR ALIGNMENT MEETING • DEBRIEF SPONSOR ALIGNMENT MEETING & REFINE PLAN

Send Materials • Review Client's Drafts • Review Client's Drafts • Prep Client & Sponsor for Meeting

5 — Coaching Sessions

COACHING SESSION • [RUN EXPERIMENTS & REFLECT • INCORPORATE RESOURCES AS NEEDED • CONNECT BETWEEN CONVERSATIONS AS NEEDED] • COACHING SESSION

MANAGE CAPACITY & SCHEDULING

OPTIONAL: Prepare Client For Session • Prep Self For Session • Reflect & Document Session • OPTIONAL: Prepare Client For Session • Prep Self For Session • Reflect & Document Session

6 — Midpoint Alignment Check

STRUCTURED MID-ENGAGEMENT ALIGNMENT DISCUSSION • (OPTIONAL: SPONSOR ALIGNMENT MEETING & DEBRIEF) • ADJUST GOALS & PLAN AS NEEDED

INFORMALLY ALIGN IN COACHING SESSIONS

Prepare Client For Alignment Discussion • (OPTIONAL: Prepare Client & Sponsor For Alignment Meeting)

7 — Closing

AGREE ON HOW/WHEN TO FINISH • (OPTIONAL: DEBRIEF PROGRESS FEEDBACK) • HARVEST LEARNINGS & CELEBRATE SUCCESS • CREATE ONGOING DEVELOPMENT PLAN • FINAL SPONSOR MEETING • FINAL COACHING SESSION

Remind Client Closing is Approaching • (OPTIONAL: Collect & Prepare Progress Feedback) • Send Materials • Prep Client & Sponsor for Final Sponsor Meeting • Honor Ending with Closing Practices

COMPLETE PROCESS CHECKLIST FROM START TO FINISH

Below is the consolidated checklist for navigating a coaching engagement from start to finish.

PUTTING YOUR BEST FOOT FORWARD: SECURING & CONTRACTING AN ENGAGEMENT

CHECKLIST: PREPARING FOR CALLS

- ❑ Do a capacity check. Do you have time to begin a new client engagement immediately? If not now, when will you be available to begin? How will you share this information with the prospective client? For a detailed discussion on managing your capacity, see *DYBC* Chapter 5.

- ❑ Review and refresh yourself on questions you may wish to ask (1-1), as well as questions you may be asked during these calls (1-2).

- ❑ Research the organization, its industry, competitors, and recent events using online tools and resources.

- ❑ Research your client (typically after an inquiry call and in advance of a chemistry call), using tools such as the organization's website and online tools like LinkedIn.

- ❑ Schedule time prior to the call to revisit the information you gathered about the organization and your client; also reserve time on your calendar immediately before the call to center yourself energetically.

- ❑ Confirm that your coaching bio is up to date so you can share it easily with the potential client prior to the call (1-3).

- ❑ If you share a sample engagement list, include any experiences relevant to your client (1-4).

CHECKLIST: POST-CALL FOLLOW-UP

- ❑ Reflect on the conversation and capture your insights and learnings, as well as any agreements and next steps (1-8).

- ❑ Share any documents that will help your client, hiring contact, or sponsor understand the coaching engagement (e.g., coaching bio, coaching process…).

❑ Send a thank-you email expressing interest and asking any follow-up questions, such as the timing of the decision.

❑ Put a future date reminder on your calendar to prompt a check-in with the individual if you have not yet heard back from them.

CHECKLIST: DRAFT THE SOW

❑ Confirm that you have the correct information for the SOW, including who it should be addressed to, where you should send it, and the timing.

❑ Before drafting the SOW, verbally confirm your approach with the hiring contact in order to avoid over- or under-delivering.

❑ Inquire about any organization-specific language or requirements that need to be addressed.

❑ Draft the SOW (1-9).

❑ Review (1-10), finalize, and send the SOW to the appropriate individual (e.g., client, hiring contact, or engagement sponsor).

❑ Follow up as needed so each party has a signed, completed SOW.

STARTING STRONG: CLIENT INTAKE & KICKOFF

CHECKLIST: SET UP ENGAGEMENT AND CLIENT SYSTEMS

❑ Create a new client file, digital or analog, and start populating it prior to your first meeting (2-1).

❑ Set up your client in your financial systems.

❑ Tailor your standard welcome email (2-2) for this new client and send it once the SOW is signed; include an overview of Roles & Responsibilities (2-3), a Coaching Agreement (2-4), and a New Client Intake Form (2-5).

CHECKLIST: THE KICKOFF MEETING

❑ Review notes from your previous conversations with your client and organization ahead of the kickoff conversation; make a note of questions you have not covered yet.

❏ Send a Kickoff Meeting email ahead of the session with your client (2-6), including your client-specific Next Steps list based on your earlier conversations with your client and the organization (2-7).

❏ Have your Coaching Process Overview (1-6) and Next Steps list (2-7) ready to share with your client during the session.

CHECKLIST: POST-KICKOFF ACTIVITIES

❏ Send your client self-reflection questions and exercises to complete ahead of the meeting (2-8 and 2-9).

❏ Schedule time in your calendar just before the Intake conversation to prepare and get present for the conversation.

❏ Review your client's materials if you've asked them to send responses ahead of the Intake conversation.

CHECKLIST: OPTIONAL: SPONSOR CONTEXT CALL

❏ Send an email (2-10) ahead of the scheduled call that includes an agenda, Coaching Process Overview (1-6), and the overview of Coaching Roles & Responsibilities (2-3).

❏ Schedule time in your calendar just before the call to prepare and get present for the conversation.

❏ During or after the call, capture agreements about how you'll work together and insights about the organizational and client context. Keep these with your client file to refer to as needed.

BUILDING AWARENESS: ASSESSMENTS

CHECKLIST: OPTIONAL: REVIEW EXISTING ASSESSMENTS

❏ Request existing assessments from your client and ask for their take on what they found useful from the assessments and what they have tried or implemented as a result of the assessments.

❏ Review any existing assessments provided by your client.

❏ Capture themes from your review to support your assessment strategy and spark your curiosity.

CHECKLIST: DEVELOP ASSESSMENT STRATEGY

❑ Consider what you have learned about your client, their organization, and objectives for the engagement during early conversations, as well as timing and desired outcomes (3-1).

❑ Determine what assessments to use for this particular client situation and explain your approach to your client.

CHECKLIST: ENGAGE CLIENT IN THE 360° ASSESSMENT PROCESS

❑ Begin by reviewing the assessment strategy with your client, including objectives, process, timing, confidentiality for all stakeholder feedback, and your client's role in the process.

❑ Have a clear, process-oriented discussion (3-2a & 3-2b) with your client that includes the following:

    ❑ Discuss considerations for selecting the colleagues they would like to participate in the 360° (3-3).

    ❑ Share the 360° Participant Tracker (3-4) with your client to capture the list and useful content information, and remind your client to review their completed list with their sponsor before finalizing it.

❑ After your client has completed the list of participants, review the list together.

❑ Confirm that their sponsor has signed off on the list of participants your client has created.

CONDUCT ASSESSMENT AND CREATE REPORT: TRACK 1: INTERVIEW-BASED 360° ASSESSMENTS

CHECKLIST: INVITE AND SCHEDULE 360° INTERVIEW PARTICIPANTS

❑ Confirm how the interviews will be scheduled and by whom.

    ❑ If working with a client's EA, talk with them about the process, share specific guidance with them, and a spreadsheet to manage the scheduling (3-4).

    ❑ If using a technology-supported approach to scheduling (e.g., Calendly), set it up appropriately before your client sends the emails inviting their participation.

❏ Share a draft email with your client that they can customize and send to participants, inviting them to participate in the 360° interviews (3-5).

❏ Once the participants have been invited to participate, scheduling can begin.

❏ Monitor the progress of the scheduling and ensure your calendar reflects all scheduled interviews; follow up as needed.

❏ Once the interview scheduling for the assessment has been completed, schedule the debrief with your client. Allow sufficient time to complete the interviews, create the assessment report materials, and prepare yourself prior to the debrief discussion.

CHECKLIST: PREPARE FOR AND INTERVIEW ASSESSMENT PARTICIPANTS

❏ Create the document you'll use for the data collected (3-6).

❏ Finalize the questions you'll use; you might wish to review these with your client and adjust accordingly.

❏ Consider how you want to introduce yourself and explain the purpose of the interview, and how you will use the collected data. Be prepared to address confidentiality concerns.

❏ Conduct the interviews, ensuring you capture data on how this colleague knows and works with your client, your client's strengths, and your client's opportunities. Be sure to collect specific examples and suggestions.

❏ Process your interviews as you go—this may mean rereading and editing or highlighting themes or questions the notes raise for you. Be mindful of not getting anchored to early interview themes.

CHECKLIST: WRITE THE ASSESSMENT REPORT

❏ Finalize key themes and supporting evidence (3-7a and 3-7b) and write the report. This may be any format you like to work with. If the report is lengthy, consider adding an executive summary that highlights the participants involved, a list of 3–4 strengths, and 2–3 opportunities.

❏ Ensure you leave enough time to write the report, step away, and come back to review it, making any refinements necessary to ensure it captures the essential feedback from the interviews.

CONDUCT ASSESSMENT AND CREATE REPORT: TRACK 2: ONLINE 360° ASSESSMENT

CHECKLIST: SET UP ONLINE 360° ASSESSMENT IN SYSTEM

- ❑ Set up a new assessment profile for your client in the online system you are using.

- ❑ Enter the required information for your client and all colleagues providing feedback.

- ❑ Adjust the start and end dates to match the timing you desire.

CHECKLIST: INVITE PARTICIPANTS AND LAUNCH ONLINE ASSESSMENT

- ❑ Notify your client that you have set up their assessment and that they can email their colleagues a request to participate. This ensures colleagues are not surprised by the assessment invitation and link that will be sent from the assessment provider once you launch the assessment.

- ❑ Your client invites colleagues via an email (3-8), with a cc to you.

- ❑ Once you receive the email (via cc), you launch the assessment to participants.

CHECKLIST: MANAGE THE ONLINE ASSESSMENT PROCESS AND CREATE REPORT

- ❑ Monitor the assessment as the deadline approaches, using reminders to encourage full participation.

- ❑ If you find that you do not have sufficient participation as you approach the deadline, move the date later and send an additional reminder.

- ❑ Close the assessment at the appropriate time and initiate the report creation.

CHECKLIST: PREPARE FOR ASSESSMENT DEBRIEF DISCUSSION

- ❑ Schedule time to prepare yourself for the debrief using a few guiding questions (3-9).

- ❑ Consider your client and how they can best explore and integrate the results; allow that to guide how and when you send the results.

- ❑ Send your client an email ahead of the debrief that prepares them to receive the debrief (3-10).

❑ Discuss your client's values and vision, which they completed in parallel with the assessment process, before debriefing their 360° assessment data. This ensures that your client's thought process is not influenced by the assessment data.

CHECKLIST: DEBRIEF RESULTS AND REFLECT ON INSIGHTS

❑ Share questions after the debrief to support your client's ongoing processing of the assessment results (3-12). Your client's responses and clarification questions can be discussed in a follow-up conversation, while key insights are captured to inform the coaching goals and plan.

❑ Capture your reflections and hunches about the debrief, making note of areas of high energy or intensity, any confusion, or resistance.

❑ In this or the next client conversation, discuss your client's choices in what to share with the sponsor and when to share it.

❑ You may wish to preview the sponsor alignment meeting as part of the conversation. We discuss this sponsor alignment meeting in Chapter 4 of this workbook.

CHARTING THE COURSE:
COACHING PLANS—VISION & GOAL SETTING

CHECKLIST: ARTICULATE CORE VALUES

❑ If you haven't yet explored your client's communication and work preferences, do so now. For example, do they prefer to reflect and write on their own, or do they prefer to think out loud and dialogue with you in real time?

❑ Discuss the exercises that will help them articulate their values and develop their vision and reinforce how this work will support your client's success (4-1 through 4-7).

❑ If your client prefers to work asynchronously, email the exercises to them.

❑ Ask your client to send their draft work prior to your session so that you can review and reflect on what they have developed.

❑ Discuss the client's values and vision before debriefing their assessment data. This ensures that the client's thought process is not influenced by the assessment data.

CHECKLIST: CREATE LEADERSHIP VISION

❑ Decide what tool you will use as you work with your client to craft their vision of the future (4-4 through 4-6).

❑ If you're using a writing exercise, email the exercise and ask your client to send their draft work prior to your session so that you can review and reflect on what they've developed.

❑ During your coaching session, support the client in drafting and refining a sentence or two that captures their future vision in a leadership vision statement (4-7).

❑ Discuss the client's vision before debriefing their assessment data. This ensures that the client's thought process is not influenced by the assessment data.

CHECKLIST: DEVELOP COACHING GOALS AND PLAN

After the Vision Statement has been created and the Assessment Debrief (see Chapter 3) has been completed:

❑ Share the coaching plan template with the client and discuss the best way to work through it (4-8a and 4-8b). As with the vision and values exercises, this will be unique to each client based on their experience and working style.

❑ Support the client to develop their goals and plan.

❑ If your client is working on this between sessions, request that they send you a draft prior to your session so you can review their draft and offer observations and questions.

CHECKLIST: SPONSOR ALIGNMENT MEETING ON COACHING GOALS AND PLAN

❑ Once the client is well underway in drafting their coaching plan, send an email (4-9) to the client's sponsor to schedule time for the alignment meeting.

❑ Review the agenda (4-10) and process (4-11) for the alignment meeting with your client and prepare them to share their themes and insights from the assessment process, as well as their coaching plan.

❑ Conduct the alignment meeting with the sponsor and client.

❑ Debrief with the client and adjust the plan if necessary.

BEING INTENTIONAL: THE COACHING SESSION

CHECKLIST: MANAGE CAPACITY AND SCHEDULING

❑ Review and update your coaching sessions tracker (5-1a) and capacity tracker (5-1b) regularly (e.g., biweekly) to ensure you are aware of your capacity.

❑ Intentionally manage new client starts to ensure your capacity is at the right level for you and your practice.

CHECKLIST: PREPARE FOR SESSION

❑ Schedule time on your calendar in advance of coaching sessions to prepare. This time may differ based on the phase of the engagement (e.g., debriefing assessments requires more preparation time).

❑ Optional: Send a pre-session preparation email to your clients (5-2).

❑ Take the time you need prior to the session to ensure you are fully present (e.g., breath work, body scan, minute of quiet). See Chapter 8 of this workbook for helpful presencing practices.

CHECKLIST: POST-SESSION DOCUMENTATION AND REFLECTION

❑ Review the session, capturing the information that is most relevant for you and your client (5-3). You may find it helpful to protect this time on your calendar after coaching sessions.

❑ Reflect on the session, considering not only what happened, but how you showed up as a coach and how you experienced your client. Note any correlations and hunches that emerge (5-4).

PAUSING TO CHECK ENGAGEMENT: MID-ENGAGEMENT ALIGNMENT

CHECKLIST: PREPARE FOR CLIENT MID-ENGAGEMENT ALIGNMENT MEETING

❑ Maintain your session tracker (5-1a) so you know when the midpoint is approaching.

❑ Let the client know that you would like the next coaching conversation to include a mid-alignment check-in (6-1).

❑ Share reflection questions ahead of the conversation so the client can prepare if they'd like to (6-1 and 6-2).

❑ Schedule time for yourself to prepare for the conversation.

❑ Prepare for the conversation: Review notes and reflections from the engagement to date, and identify progress, challenges, and possible improvements.

CHECKLIST: CLIENT MID-ENGAGEMENT ALIGNMENT MEETING FOLLOW-UP

❑ Note any changes agreed to and take appropriate actions (e.g., changing timing or cadence of meetings; sending reflection questions ahead of calls, or not).

CHECKLIST: PREPARE FOR SPONSOR MID-ENGAGEMENT ALIGNMENT MEETING

❑ Discuss and prepare for the meeting with your client

❑ Agree with your client as to who will schedule the sponsor meeting and who will send an email about the meeting to the sponsor (6-3)

❑ Once the sponsor meeting is scheduled, also schedule a follow-up debrief conversation with your client

CHECKLIST: DEBRIEF SPONSOR MID-ENGAGEMENT ALIGNMENT MEETING

❑ Review the conversation with your client—what did they think and feel about the conversation, and what did they learn from the discussion that they want to capture in their goals or plan?

CHECKLIST: ADJUST GOALS AND PLAN AS NEEDED

❑ Support the client in revising their goals and plan as they see fit based on the coach-client alignment discussion and possibly the sponsor mid-engagement alignment meeting.

❑ Agree on how and with whom to communicate any revisions. We encourage client ownership of the goals and plan document and therefore suggest they communicate any changes.

FINISHING STRONG:
CLOSING A COACHING ENGAGEMENT

CHECKLIST: REMIND CLIENT THAT CLOSING IS APPROACHING

❑ Maintain your session tracker so you are aware of the timing for initiating closing activities.

❑ When you're 4–6 weeks from closing, let the client know that the end is approaching and discuss the activities that create a strong close. You may choose to email your client in advance of the discussion and share the topics to be covered (7-1).

CHECKLIST: OPTIONAL: COLLECT, PREPARE, AND DEBRIEF PROGRESS FEEDBACK

❑ If you've agreed to collect progress feedback as part of closing, decide the following with your client:

❑ What subset of stakeholders will be involved and who will invite them to participate (7-2)?

❑ How to phrase the coaching goals during the interviews.

❑ After collecting the feedback, summarize the results to share with the client (7-3a and 7-3b).

❑ Prepare to share the feedback in the same way you prepare to deliver 360° feedback (see Chapter 3).

CHECKLIST: SEND MATERIALS TO HARVEST LEARNINGS AND CELEBRATE SUCCESS

❑ Create a set of reflection questions appropriate for the client and the work you've done together (7-4).

❑ Send reflection questions with plenty of time for your client to complete the work, and invite them to share their reflections with you in advance of the session.

❑ Review your client's reflections and consider where you may have additional observations of progress that you can share during the discussion.

❑ Discuss learnings and celebrate!

CHECKLIST: CREATE ONGOING DEVELOPMENT PLAN

❑ Review your notes and experiences of the client engagement, identifying the key themes, shifts, learnings, and your hunches for the client's ongoing development areas.

❑ Support the client in reviewing their leadership vision, coaching plan, progress feedback (if collected), and learnings about themselves as they consider how they'd like to continue development after coaching ends.

❑ Offer the client a structure to capture their Ongoing Development Plan (7-5).

CHECKLIST: PREPARE CLIENT FOR AND HAVE FINAL SPONSOR MEETING

❑ Prepare your client for the final sponsor meeting (7-6).

❑ Customize the agenda for the final sponsor meeting (7-7).

❑ Email an overview of the meeting (7-8) to the sponsor, outlining the objectives; your client can include any supporting materials they wish to share (e.g., reflection highlights, ongoing development plan, progress feedback).

❑ Support your client and the sponsor in having the wrap-up conversation (per earlier sponsor conversations).

CHECKLIST: FINAL COACHING SESSION

❑ Debrief the sponsor meeting with your client—key takeaways, refinements to the plan, next steps.

❑ Ensure there is time to honor your client's progress and appreciate the time you have had together.

❑ Agree on any follow-on and expectations of one another now that the coaching engagement has wrapped up.

❑ Optional: Ask your client for feedback so you can understand what you've done well and where you could have been even more impactful as the coach.

CHECKLIST: HONOR THE ENDING WITH COACH CLOSING PRACTICES

❑ Create time to go through your own closing ritual or process for an engagement (7-9)—which may include both reflective activities and process activities (e.g., send a final invoice or close out the client on the tracker).

YOUR PRESENCE IS AN INTERVENTION: COACHING PRESENCE

CHECKLIST: DEVELOPING YOUR PRESENCE

- ☐ Assess your presence as it is today (8-1).

- ☐ If you feel you have a well-developed presence and supporting practices, consider how to sustain and strengthen your presence and practices (see Resources).

- ☐ If you would like to further develop your presence and supporting practices:

    - ○ Complete the additional reflection questions below (8-2).

    - ○ Explore supporting practices that feel consistent with who you are and identify 1–3 practices you wish to experiment with.

    - ○ Create experiments with new practices, and adjust your approach based on your experiences.

CHECKLIST: PRESENCE BEFORE, DURING AND AFTER COACHING CONVERSATIONS

- ☐ Schedule time to prepare and get present before every coaching session (8-5 and 8-6).

- ☐ Practice centering and presence during coaching sessions (8-7).

- ☐ Schedule time to regroup and re-center after a session (8-8).

YOU ARE YOUR OWN BEST TOOL: ONGOING DEVELOPMENT

CHECKLIST: ONGOING DEVELOPMENT: REFLECT, REVIEW AND INTEGRATE

- ☐ Document your learning journey to date or update an existing version to offer a holistic perspective on how you have invested in yourself and what has or hasn't had impact (9-1).

- ☐ Reflect on the past year and mine insights from your client engagements to provide possible directions for development (9-2).

- ☐ Revisit your reflections on who you are as a coach and your vision (see Building the Foundation earlier in the workbook and 9-4).

❑ Notice what remains true and where new interests may be emerging (9-4).

❑ Review practical considerations that may influence your development decisions (e.g., are there tools or frameworks a client organization would like you to use?).

❑ Bring it all together.

CHECKLIST: ONGOING DEVELOPMENT: IDEATE AND RESEARCH

❑ Identify the development categories and programs that will support you in moving toward your vision of who you want to be as a coach and your ideal practice (9-5).

❑ Research possible programs and experiences that support your vision and your practice (9-6 and 9-7).

CHECKLIST: ONGOING DEVELOPMENT: STRATEGIZE AND PLAN

❑ Create your development plan for the year ahead. Consider what times of year are best for you to carve out for your development, especially if you want to undertake an intensive learning experience (9-8).

TOOLS, TEMPLATES AND EXAMPLES:
TOOLS YOU'LL FIND IN THE WORKBOOK
FROM START TO FINISH

START HERE

Building the Foundation—Coach Self-Reflection

Building the Foundation—Vision Statement

PUTTING YOUR BEST FOOT FORWARD: SECURING A COACHING ENGAGEMENT

1-1 Questions You May Wish to Ask During an Inquiry Call

1-2 Questions You Should Be Prepared to Answer During an Inquiry Call

1-3 Coach Biography

1-4 Recent Coaching Engagements

1-5 Chemistry Call Approach

1-6 Coaching Process Overview

1-7 Getting Present Before a Call

1-8 Post-Call Reflection Questions

1-9 Draft the SOW

1-10 SOW Review Questions

STARTING STRONG: CLIENT INTAKE AND KICKOFF

2-1 Set Up New Engagement and Client File

2-2 Welcome and Getting Started Email

2-3 Overview of Roles & Responsibilities

2-4 Sample Coach-Client Agreement

2-5 New Client Form

2-6 New Client Kickoff Meeting Email

BUILDING AWARENESS: ASSESSMENTS

CHARTING THE COURSE: COACHING PLANS – VISION AND GOAL SETTING

BEING INTENTIONAL: THE COACHING SESSION

PAUSING TO CHECK CONNECTION: MID-ENGAGEMENT ALIGNMENT

FINISHING STRONG: CLOSING A COACHING ENGAGEMENT

YOUR PRESENCE IS AN INTERVENTION: COACHING PRESENCE

YOU ARE YOUR OWN BEST TOOL: ONGOING DEVELOPMENT FOR COACHES

COACH REFLECTION QUESTIONS

As coaches we know the importance of regular reflection, so we have included an additional set of reflection worksheets to support this practice.

BUILDING THE FOUNDATION—COACH SELF-REFLECTION AND VISION STATEMENT

WHO AM I AS A COACH TODAY?
What is my coaching philosophy?

What are my strengths as a coach?

What are my learning edges?

WHO DO I WANT TO BE AS A COACH IN THE FUTURE?
What aspects of my coaching philosophy do I wish to evolve?

What strengths do I want to bring forward?

What types of development will support my intentional growth?

HOW DO I WORK AS A COACH TODAY?

Reflect back on the past 12 months as you answer the following questions:

What is important to me about my current coaching approach?

What is important to my clients about this approach?

What do I like about my current coaching process/approach?

Where did I do my best work? What made it my best, and what conditions enabled it?

What, if any, recurring sticky situations did I face that could be prevented or minimized by altering my approach?

What does my portfolio of work look like (e.g., types of work, organizations and/or leaders)?

What clients do I most enjoy working with? Why?

What clients do I prefer to avoid? Why?

What types of organizations do I most enjoy working with? Why?

What types of organizations do I prefer to avoid? Why?

Do I have the right amount of work and/or number of clients to have a meaningful and sustainable coaching practice consistent with the life I want to lead?

HOW DO I WANT TO WORK AS A COACH IN THE FUTURE?
What would I like to change or experiment with in my current process/approach?

Are there any new coaching modalities or tools that I'd like to explore? If so, what draws me to them?

What types of clients or organizations am I feeling drawn to?

Am I feeling "done" with any particular types of clients or organizations? If so, what types or organizations?

How might I want to increase or decrease the amount of work and/or number of clients I have in order to have a meaningful and sustainable coaching practice consistent with the life I want to lead?

ENVISION YOUR FUTURE

What do I want my life to look like in the years ahead?

How does work fit into that vision?

Who do I want to be as a coach in the years ahead?

What type of work do I want to be doing, with whom, and where?

NOW CREATE YOUR VISION STATEMENT

Once you have created a compelling vision of your desired future as a coach, capture the essence of it in a sentence or two. Below is an example you can use as a model.

Vision Statement Example

I work with vibrant leaders and changemakers who are passionate about growing their impact and leading their organizations to new heights of excellence. My clients love learning, are willing to experiment in order to grow, and work with me for 6- to 12-month engagements.

Date: January 13, 2023

My Vision Statement:

COACH YEAR IN REVIEW REFLECTION QUESTIONS

Review and reflect on the last 12 months. You may consider referencing resources such as Pamela McLean's Self as Coach model (9-3) and the ICF and/or EMCC Competencies models to ensure that you consider multiple aspects of your work as a coach (see Appendix):

What are you most proud of this year? Why?

What (if anything) makes you wish you could have a "do-over"? Why?

Are there any "sticky situations" that you noticed coming up repeatedly?

Where do you think you are strongest as a coach today?

Where do you see opportunities to develop?

What insights have you gained from the feedback you've received?

What aspects of coaching are you curious to learn more about? Why?

What aspects of coaching are you prepared to leave behind? Why?

LEARNING DEVELOPMENT IDEATION EXERCISE

Now that you have a clear view of your learning journey, the insights you have harvested, and a clear vision for the year ahead, bring them together and consider what type of development will support your journey to achieving your vision:

Where do I want to take my coaching practice in the next few years, and what learning will support me in achieving this vision?

What feedback am I getting from clients about my coaching and how can that inform my development plan?

What development will make me a better coach for my clients moving forward?

What tools or frameworks have I heard about from colleagues or research that have piqued my curiosity?

Are there tools or frameworks that client organizations (or my organization) would like me to use?

What time, energy, and money can I devote to my development this year?

How do I need to pace my learning activities, given my personal and professional commitments in the year(s) ahead?

What are the opportunities to learn with my colleagues and build community?

What topics are most interesting to me right now?

ICF AND EMCC COMPETENCIES (2020)

Coaching competencies have been established by governance and thought leadership bodies in the field of coaching, including the International Coaching Federation (ICF) and the European Mentoring and Coaching Council (EMCC). We've included them here for reference as you reflect on your coaching and plan for your ongoing development. For a deeper dive into any of these competencies, the tables offer suggested chapters in *DYBC*.

ICF COMPETENCIES

ICF COMPETENCY	SUGGESTED CHAPTER

A. Foundation
1. Demonstrates Ethical Practice
Definition: Understands and consistently applies coaching ethics and standards of coaching
    1. Demonstrates personal integrity and honesty in interactions with clients, sponsors and relevant stakeholders
    2. Is sensitive to clients' identity, environment, experiences, values and beliefs
    3. Uses language appropriate and respectful to clients, sponsors and relevant stakeholders
    4. Abides by the ICF Code of Ethics and upholds the Core Values
    5. Maintains confidentiality with client information per stakeholder agreements and pertinent laws
    6. Maintains the distinctions between coaching, consulting, psychotherapy and other support professions
    7. Refers clients to other support professionals, as appropriate
	Establishing and maintaining confidentiality with sponsors and stakeholders:
	
	Chapter 1: Putting Your Best Foot Forward
	
	Chapter 2: Starting Strong
	
	Chapter 3: Building Awareness

Foundation
2. Embodies a Coaching Mindset
Definition: Develops and maintains a mindset that is open, curious, flexible and client-centered
    1. Acknowledges that clients are responsible for their own choices
    2. Engages in ongoing learning and development as a coach
    3. Develops an ongoing reflective practice to enhance one's coaching
    4. Remains aware of and open to the influence of context and culture on self and others
    5. Uses awareness of self and one's intuition to benefit clients
    6. Develops and maintains the ability to regulate one's emotions
    7. Mentally and emotionally prepares for sessions
    8. Seeks help from outside sources when necessary
	Reflective practices and session preparation:
	
	Chapter 5: Being Intentional
	
	Chapter 8: Your Presence Is An Intervention
	
	Ongoing development: for Coaches:
	
	Chapter 9: You Are Your Own Best Tool

ICF COMPETENCY	SUGGESTED CHAPTER
B. Co-Creating the Relationship *3. Establishes and Maintains Agreements* Definition: Partners with the client and relevant stakeholders to create clear agreements about the coaching relationship, process, plans and goals. Establishes agreements for the overall coaching engagement as well as those for each coaching session. 1. Explains what coaching is and is not and describes the process to the client and relevant stakeholders 2. Reaches agreement about what is and is not appropriate in the relationship, what is and is not being offered, and the responsibilities of the client and relevant stakeholders 3. Reaches agreement about the guidelines and specific parameters of the coaching relationship such as logistics, fees, scheduling, duration, termination, confidentiality and inclusion of others 4. Partners with the client and relevant stakeholders to establish an overall coaching plan and goals 5. Partners with the client to determine client-coach compatibility 6. Partners with the client to identify or reconfirm what they want to accomplish in the session 7. Partners with the client to define what the client believes they need to address or resolve to achieve what they want to accomplish in the session	Guidance establishing and maintaining agreements across the coaching engagement: Chapter 1: Putting Your Best Foot Forward Chapter 2: Starting Strong Chapter 3: Building Awareness Chapter 4: Charting the Course Chapter 5: Being Intentional Chapter 7: Finishing Strong
8. Partners with the client to define or reconfirm measures of success for what the client wants to accomplish in the coaching engagement or individual session 9. Partners with the client to manage the time and focus of the session 10. Continues coaching in the direction of the client's desired outcome unless the client indicates otherwise 11. Partners with the client to end the coaching relationship in a way that honors the experience	Guidance establishing and maintaining agreements across the coaching engagement: Chapter 1: Putting Your Best Foot Forward Chapter 2: Starting Strong Chapter 3: Building Awareness Chapter 4: Charting the Course Chapter 5: Being Intentional Chapter 7: Finishing Strong

ICF COMPETENCY	SUGGESTED CHAPTER
B. Co-Creating the Relationship *4. Cultivates Trust and Safety* Definition: Partners with the client to create a safe, supportive environment that allows the client to share freely. Maintains a relationship of mutual respect and trust. 1. Seeks to understand the client within their context, which may include their identity, environment, experiences, values and beliefs 2. Demonstrates respect for the client's identity, perceptions, style and language and adapts one's coaching to the client 3. Acknowledges and respects the client's unique talents, insights and work in the coaching process 4. Shows support, empathy and concern for the client 5. Acknowledges and supports the client's expression of feelings, perceptions, concerns, beliefs and suggestions 6. Demonstrates openness and transparency as a way to display vulnerability and build trust with the client	Creating a trust-based relationship and the safe space for clients to do their work: Chapter 2: Starting Strong Chapter 5: Being Intentional
B. Co-Creating the Relationship *5. Maintains Presence* Definition: Is fully conscious and present with the client, employing a style that is open, flexible, grounded and confident 1. Remains focused, observant, empathetic and responsive to the client 2. Demonstrates curiosity during the coaching process 3. Manages one's emotions to stay present with the client 4. Demonstrates confidence in working with strong client emotions during the coaching process 5. Is comfortable working in a space of not knowing 6. Creates or allows space for silence, pause or reflection	Presence during specific points of the engagement: Chapter 3: Building Awareness Chapter 5: Being Intentional Developing coaching presence: Chapter 8: Your Presence Is an Intervention

ICF COMPETENCY	SUGGESTED CHAPTER

C. Communicating Effectively
6. Listens Actively
Definition: Focuses on what the client is and is not saying to fully understand what is being communicated in the context of the client systems and to support client self-expression
   1. Considers the client's context, identity, environment, experiences, values and beliefs to enhance understanding of what the client is communicating
   2. Reflects or summarizes what the client communicated to ensure clarity and understanding
   3. Recognizes and inquires when there is more to what the client is communicating
   4. Notices, acknowledges and explores the client's emotions, energy shifts, nonverbal cues or other behaviors
   5. Integrates the client's words, tone of voice and body language to determine the full meaning of what is being communicated
   6. Notices trends in the client's behaviors and emotions across sessions to discern themes and patterns
	Active listening:
	
	Chapter 2: Starting Strong
	
	Chapter 5: Being Intentional
	
	Chapter 8: Your Presence Is An Intervention

C. Communicating Effectively
7. Evokes Awareness
Definition: Facilitates client insight and learning by using tools and techniques such as powerful questioning, silence, metaphor or analogy
   1. Considers client experience when deciding what might be most useful
   2. Challenges the client as a way to evoke awareness or insight
   3. Asks questions about the client, such as their way of thinking, values, needs, wants and beliefs
   4. Asks questions that help the client explore beyond current thinking
   5. Invites the client to share more about their experience in the moment
   6. Notices what is working to enhance client progress
   7. Adjusts the coaching approach in response to the client's needs
   8. Helps the client identify factors that influence current and future patterns of behavior, thinking or emotion
   9. Invites the client to generate ideas about how they can move forward and what they are willing or able to do
   10. Supports the client in reframing perspectives
   11. Shares observations, insights and feelings, without attachment, that have the potential to create new learning for the client
	Evoking awareness in clients by creating the right conditions:
	
	Chapter 3: Building Awareness
	
	Chapter 4: Charting the Course
	
	Chapter 5: Being Intentional
	
	Chapter 6: Pausing to Check Connection

ICF COMPETENCY	SUGGESTED CHAPTER
D. Cultivating Learning and Growth *8. Facilitates Client Growth* Definition: Partners with the client to transform learning and insight into action. Promotes client autonomy in the coaching process. 　1. Works with the client to integrate new awareness, insight or learning into their worldview and behaviors 　2. Partners with the client to design goals, actions and accountability measures that integrate and expand new learning 　3. Acknowledges and supports client autonomy in the design of goals, actions and methods of accountability 　4. Supports the client in identifying potential results or learning from identified action steps 　5. Invites the client to consider how to move forward, including resources, support and potential barriers 　6. Partners with the client to summarize learning and insight within or between sessions 　7. Celebrates the client's progress and successes 　8. Partners with the client to close the session	Using assessments to generate new learning: Chapter 3: Building Awareness Chapter 3+: 360° Assessments Designing goals and success measures: Chapter 4: Charting the Course Preparing clients for learning in and from sessions: Chapter 5: Being Intentional Recognizing and celebrating progress: Chapter 7: Finishing Strong

EMCC COMPETENCES
EIGHT COACHING / MENTORING COMPETENCE CATEGORIES

CATEGORY	DESCRIPTION	RECOMMENDED CHAPTER
1. Understanding Self	Demonstrates awareness of own values, beliefs and behaviours; recognises how these affect their practice and uses this self-awareness to manage their effectiveness in meeting the client's, and where relevant, the sponsor's objectives	Understanding self as coach and the impact on the coaching engagement: Chapter 5: Being Intentional Chapter 6: Pausing to Check Connection Chapter 7: Finishing Strong Chapter 8: Your Presence Is an Intervention Chapter 9: You Are Your Own Best Tool
2. Commitment to Self-Development	Explore and improve the standard of their practice and maintain the reputation of the profession	Ongoing development for Coaches: Chapter 9: You Are Your Own Best Tool
3. Managing the Contract	Establishes and maintains the expectations and boundaries of the mentoring/coaching contract with the client and, where appropriate, with sponsors	Expectations, boundaries, and contracting: Chapter 1: Putting Your Best Foot Forward Chapter 2: Starting Strong Chapter 4: Charting the Course Chapter 6: Pausing to Check Connection Chapter 7: Finishing Strong
4. Building the Relationship	Skillfully builds and maintains an effective relationship with the client, and where appropriate, with the sponsor	Building and maintaining effective relationships over the course of the coaching engagement: Chapter 2: Starting Strong Chapter 5: Being Intentional Chapter 6: Pausing to Check Connection Chapter 7: Finishing Strong
5. Enabling Insight and Learning	Works with the client and sponsor to bring about insight and learning	Creating the container for client and sponsor insight and learning: Chapter 3: Building Awareness Chapter 4: Charting the Course Chapter 5: Being Intentional Chapter 6: Pausing to Check Connection Chapter 7: Finishing Strong
6. Outcome and Action Orientation	Demonstrates approach and uses the skills in supporting the client to make desired changes	Chapter 4: Charting the Course, Chapter 5: Being Intentional, Chapter 6: Pausing to Check Connection, and Chapter 7: Finishing Strong all support taking an outcome and action orientation to coaching work, working with clients to make their desired changes.

EMCC COMPETENCES
EIGHT COACHING / MENTORING COMPETENCE CATEGORIES

CATEGORY	DESCRIPTION	RECOMMENDED CHAPTER
7. Use of Models and Techniques	Applies models and tools, techniques, and ideas beyond the core communication skills in order to bring about insight and learning	Using tools and techniques beyond core communication skills: Chapter 3: Building Awareness Chapter 5: Being Intentional Bringing about insight at the mid-engagement and closing points: Chapter 6: Pausing to Check Connection Chapter 7: Finishing Strong
8. Evaluation	Gathers information on the effectiveness of own practice and contributes to establishing a culture of evaluation of outcomes.	Setting an engagement up to include the expectation and explanation of evaluation: Chapter 1: Putting Your Best Foot Forward Chapter 2: Starting Strong Soliciting feedback for the coach as well as the client: Chapter 5: Being Intentional Chapter 6: Pausing to Check Connection Chapter 7: Finishing Strong Stepping back to evaluate one's work as a coach: Chapter 9: You Are Your Own Best Tool

NOTES

ABOUT US

JULIE HESS

For more than 25 years, Julie Hess has worked with leaders, teams, and organizations to achieve breakthrough results.

Julie began her career in the industrial plastics industry, working with global clients to solve complex design and manufacturing challenges. During this time she identified an untapped market for existing materials that she subsequently developed into her firm's fastest-growing business unit.

Later, she took her passion for problem-solving into the world of corporate and organizational strategy, first at consulting firm CSC Index and later as an executive in Motorola's Leadership and Organization Effectiveness Group. It was here that Julie developed her passion for coaching, which led her to complete her initial coaching certification at the Hudson Institute of Santa Barbara, a pioneer in coach education and development. In 2001, Julie founded Catalyst Consulting and has continuously led and grown the practice since.

Today, Julie divides her time between her executive coaching practice and supporting the development of other coaches as a Coach Supervisor and educator. Her broad background enables her to fully appreciate the challenges that her coaching clients and their organizations face. Julie has worked with clients in a broad range of industries including technology, healthcare, consumer packaged goods, pharmaceuticals, hospitality, automotive, financial services, professional services, and real estate. She is known as an authentic, thoughtful, and direct partner to her clients, helping them to achieve the growth they desire.

Julie holds an MBA from the Kellogg Graduate School of Business and a Master of Engineering Management from the McCormick School of Engineering at Northwestern University, and a BS in Business Administration from DePaul University. She earned her diploma in Coach Supervision from the Coaching Supervision Academy and holds a PCC from the International Coach Federation.

Julie lives in Chicago, Illinois, and Naples, Florida, with her best coach, her husband Dan, and their two dogs Noodle and Mousse.

This is Julie's second book. Her first book, also co-authored with Laura, is *Do Your Best Coaching: Navigating An Engagement From Start To Finish*.

LAURA DALEY

Laura is an executive coach, leadership advisor, and strategy consultant with more than 25 years of experience. Over the past decade, she has coached hundreds of executives in industries including private equity, technology, financial services, biopharma, and nonprofits. Laura is direct and empathetic, combining practical business perspective with an appreciation for the challenges leaders face as they develop new ways of thinking and working.

Having experienced all sides of coaching, Laura brings a broad perspective and appreciation for her clients and their organizational systems. At Spencer Stuart, as Vice President of Learning & Development, she supported firm leaders through coaching. In building The Goodstone Group, she grew the coach network and partnered with clients to match coaches to their needs. Today, Laura serves as an external coach and advisor, working with executives, leadership teams, and coaches-in-training.

Laura's first career was management consulting, working for Katzenbach Partners, Scient, Gemini Consulting, and American Management Systems. She consulted across industries and functions, worked with start-ups, midsize companies, and multinationals, and traveled the world for clients in North America, Europe, Africa, and Asia. She holds an MBA with honors from UCLA Anderson, a BA with honors in Economics and International Relations from Cornell University, and a PCC from the International Coach Federation. She studied at the Hudson Institute of Coaching, the Graduate Institute, Geneva, and HEC Paris.

Laura enjoys learning and drawing inspiration from her husband, Alec, and daughter, Maddie, as well as her clients, movement, and travel.

This is the second book Laura co-authored with Julie. Their first is *Do Your Best Coaching: Navigating An Engagement From Start To Finish.*